P9-EFG-682

796.91
H/L

$14.95

BC # 24985

12-95

76(?)

796.91
H/L.

DATE DUE

I.L.L. 96/97
MR 07 '06

GAYLORD   PRINTED IN U.S.A.

A *Sports Illustrated For Kids* Book

Blairsville High School Library

Copyright © 1991 by The Time Inc. Magazine Company

All rights reserved. No part of this book may be reproduced in any form or by any electronic or mechanical means, including information storage and retrieval systems, without permission in writing from the publisher, except by a reviewer who may quote brief passages in a review.

First Edition

Library of Congress Cataloging-in-Publication Data

Hilgers, Laura.

Great skates/Laura Hilgers. — 1st ed.

p. cm.

"A sports illustrated for kids book."

Summary: Describes the beginnings, challenges, disappointments, and triumphs of prominent men and women in the sport of figure skating.

ISBN 0-316-36240-9

1. Skaters — Biography — Juvenile literature. [1. Skaters.]

I. Title.

GV850.A2H55   1991

796.91'2'0922 — dc20   91-14764

[B]

SPORTS ILLUSTRATED FOR KIDS is a trademark of The Time Inc. Magazine Company.

Sports Illustrated For Kids Books is an imprint of Little, Brown and Company.

10 9 8 7 6 5 4 3 2 1

RRD OH

For further information regarding this title, write to Little, Brown and Company, 34 Beacon Street, Boston, MA 02108

Published simultaneously in Canada by Little, Brown and Company (Canada) Limited

Printed in the United States of America

Design by Pegi Goodman

Contents

GLOSSARY 4

INTRODUCTION 7

CHAPTER 1   **Sonja Henie** 9

CHAPTER 2   **Dick Button** 14

CHAPTER 3   **Tenley Albright** 19

CHAPTER 4   **David and Hayes Jenkins** 24

CHAPTER 5   **Carol Heiss** 29

CHAPTER 6   **Maribel Vinson Owen** 34

CHAPTER 7   **Peggy Fleming** 39

CHAPTER 8   **John Curry** 44

CHAPTER 9   **Dorothy Hamill** 49

CHAPTER 10   **Robin Cousins** 54

CHAPTER 11   **Scott Hamilton** 59

CHAPTER 12   **Brian Boitano** 64

CHAPTER 13   **Katarina Witt** 69

CHAPTER 14   **Debi Thomas** 74

PAIRS SKATING 79

CHAPTER 15   **The Protopopovs** 80

CHAPTER 16   **Irina Rodnina and Partners** 85

CHAPTER 17   **Torvill and Dean** 90

Glossary

Arabesque (also called spiral): a skating position borrowed from ballet, in which one leg is extended up and backward.

Axel: a jump made as the skater moves forward. In this move a skater jumps off one foot, turns one and a half times in the air, and lands on the opposite foot, skating backward. The jump is named for Axel Paulsen, who introduced it in the early 1900s.

Axel

Backward: the direction used by skaters to begin most of their jumps. Skaters are moving backward when they head in the direction their backs face. Skating directions refer only to the skater; they do not involve the skater's relationship to the positions of either the audience or the judges at rinkside.

Camel Spin: a spin in the spiral or arabesque position, with one leg extended backward. The arms are often outstretched. A flying camel is a jump onto the

camel spin

other foot and then into the camel spin.

Choreography: the arrangement of required jumps, spins, and other skating moves to music of the skater's choice for presentation in figure skating and ice dancing competitions.

Compulsory Figures (also called the school figures or figures): the set patterns upon which figure skating is based; a group of 41 patterns that derive from the two-circle "figure eight" move. In past competitions, skaters had to carve selected figures into the ice with their skates a set number of times, after which judges inspected the resulting marks on the ice for the figure's precision and awarded a score. In the 1991 season, compulsory figures were eliminated from the singles competition and became a separate event.

death spiral

Cross-foot Spin: a move in which the skater crosses one leg over the other while spinning.

Death Spiral: a maneuver performed in pairs skating in which the man pivots in place while holding the outstretched arm of the woman, who spirals around him, while leaning backward and parallel to the ice, supported on one skate.

Edge: either the inside or outside portion of the skate blade.

Figure Skates: Figure skates have two distinct edges on their blades. The two edges—along with the gentle curve of the blade from front to back—make figure skates ideal for skating circles, because the skater can lean on either edge. Figure skates also have a toe pick, which aids in performing jumps and spins. Hockey skates have only one edge on their blades and no toe pick.

Flip Jump: a simple jump in which the skater skates backward, jumps off one foot, makes a full turn in the air, and lands on the same foot.

Forward: refers to the direction the skater is moving; it does not refer to the position of the audience or the judges in relation to the skater.

Free Skating (also called the freestyle or long program): the part of the competition in which each skater performs a choreographed routine, usually including a series of jumps, spins, and other

moves to music. Two sets of scores are given for free skating; one set is for technical merit, the other is for artistic impression. The free skating program now counts for two thirds of a skater's total score. For women, this program is four minutes long. For the men, it is four and one half minutes long.

Grand Slam: refers to a skater or skating couple winning all the major competitions in a single skating season. In an Olympic year, this would include

the nationals, the worlds, and the Olympics.

Ice Dancing: a two-part event in which couples perform ballroom-type dances on skates to music. There are specific rules limiting the kinds of jumps, lifts, and amount of time the partners can be apart. In competitions, ice dancing skaters receive two sets of scores—one for technical merit and the second for artistic presentation.

Judge: an official who evaluates the performance of each skater or skating pair.

Layback Spin: a spin performed on one foot. During the spin, the skater arches the back and often raises the arms and the free leg.

layback spin

Lift: a move in pairs skating and ice dancing in which the man raises the woman off the ice.

Lutz

Lutz: a difficult jump in which the skater begins by skating backward, jumps and makes a full turn in the opposite direction of the original curve. The skater lands on the other foot, gliding backwards.

Original Dance: an event in ice dancing competitions in which all couples perform the same dance, but to music of their choice. The dance, selected by the judges and announced before a specific competition, is then known as that season's Original Set Pattern. Judges give two sets of scores after each couple has performed this two-and-a-half minute work. This event counts for 30 percent of the couple's total score. (The free skating routine counts for 70 percent.)

Original Program (also known as the short program): a two-minute-and-forty-second program during which singles skaters execute eight required freestyle moves—such as a double Axel jump or a flying sit spin—to music of the individual's choice. Skaters receive two sets of scores for the short program; one for required elements and one for artistic impression. The short program counts for one third of a skater's total score.

Presentation (also known as artistic impression): refers to the way a skater interprets and moves to the music and the style in which the program is skated. The best skaters don't skate from jump to jump; they choreograph their program with moves that complement the music.

Salchow: a basic jump in which the skater, moving backward, jumps off one foot, makes a full turn in the air, and lands on the other foot. It was originated by Ulrich Salchow, who won the first men's figure skating gold medal, at the 1908 Olympics in London.

Shadow Skating: any movement or series of moves in pairs skating performed by both partners at the same time, while skating close to each other.

sit spin

Sit Spin: a spin in a squatting position, on one skate, usually with the free leg stretched out in front of the body. A flying sit spin starts with a jump.

Split Jump: a jump during which the skater kicks his or her legs up and out to each side as if to do a split in the air.

Spread Eagle: a two-foot glide in which both feet are on the same edge of the skate blade, either inside or outside, with the heels facing each other and the toes pointing out.

Toe Loop Jump: a simple jump often used in between more difficult jumps or spins. The skater glides backward and begins by using the toe of one foot to push off the ice to help gain height, then revolves once in the air, and lands on the other foot, gliding backward.

spread eagle

Two-footed Spin: a beginner's spin, done with both blades on the ice.

Salchow

Introduction

The spectacular leaps of Brian Boitano. The exquisite grace of Katarina Witt. Those are the thrilling sights that people remember when they think of Olympic figure skating.

Figure skating was introduced as an Olympic sport in 1908, and has been the highlight of the Winter Games since the Olympics were split into separate winter and summer competitions in 1924. The sport has grown and changed a lot since then, and today, it is more popular than ever.

Figure skating appeals to so many people because the skaters are more than great athletes; they are also performers. They dress up as though they were on a

HEINZ KLUETMEIR/SPORTS ILLUSTRATED

In the 1988 Olympics, Debi Thomas skated with athleticism and flair to music from the opera, "Carmen."

stage and skate a program they hope will please the audience as well as the judges. Skaters even receive two scores from the judges for their performances: one is for technical merit and the other for artistic impression.

Skaters make the most difficult acrobatic spins and gravity-defying jumps look so easy, but the ease with which they perform is the result of many years of practice. Figure skating is a difficult, demanding sport. Most world-class skaters skate a minimum of six hours a day for at least 10 years before they qualify to compete in the Olympics.

Until 1991, much of that practice was on

the compulsory figures, which are patterns—like the "figure eight"—that skaters trace slowly on the ice. The compulsory figures were all that skaters were judged on when the sport first became popular in the 1800s in Northern Europe, particularly in England and Austria.

In 1864, however, Jackson Haines, a ballet dancer from New York City, traveled overseas and showed the Europeans that there could be more to figure skating than making figure eights on the ice. Haines danced on the ice to music, and what we now call free skating was born.

Although compulsory figures remained a major part of figure skating competition, over the years they became less and less important. When the great champion Sonja Henie was skating in the 1920s and 1930s, compulsory figures counted for 60 percent of the total score. In 1968, the figures were worth 50 percent, and in 1976, they were reduced to 30 percent. Then, beginning with the 1991 season, compulsory figures were taken out of singles competition altogether. In some local competitions, they remain as a separate event.

Most figure skating fans were happy to see the compulsory figures eliminated; they were no fun to watch. Audiences wanted to see skaters perform the new jumps, spins, and graceful dance movements that were being introduced to the sport all through this century.

Today, a singles figure skating competition consists of both an original program (previously called a short program), and a long, free skating program. The original program, which now counts for one third of the total score, is made up of specific required moves, skated to music selected by the skaters. But in the free skating program, which now counts for two thirds, skaters can show off their most daring jumps and spins as well as their own style. It is the most spectacular and popular event in figure skating. Great skaters are almost always remembered for their free skating performances.

While the Olympics is the most widely-watched figure skating competition, it is not the only one. Every year, skaters all over the world compete in their own country at many levels—from the juvenile (for skaters under age 13) through the intermediate, novice, junior, and senior ranks (based on ability, not age) to regional and sectional championships, leading all the way up to the national and international championships. Every skater featured in this book started out competing as a child and progressed step by step. And every one became a national, a world or an Olympic champion.

Most people know these great skaters through their Olympic performances. Few long-time skating fans can forget the crowd-pleasing style of 1928, 1932, and 1936 champion Sonja Henie, the acrobatic leaps of 1948 and 1952 champion Dick Button, the elegance of 1964 champion Peggy Fleming, the athleticism of 1984 champion Scott Hamilton, or the charm of 1984 and 1988 champion Katarina Witt.

Great Skates features the stories of those and other great figure skating champions, who used their talent and imagination to advance the sport to a higher level. In doing so, they all helped to make figure skating the exciting sport it is today.

CHAPTER 1

Sonja Henie

With her short skirts and long jumps, she woke up a sleepy sport

Sonja Henie [*sahn-YA HEN-ee*] is often called the greatest woman figure skater of all time. From 1927 through 1936, she won 10 world championships and 3 Olympic gold medals —that's almost everything she possibly could have won in her sport!

But Sonja did more than win medals; she changed the sport of figure skating. Before she came onto the scene, figure skating was a dull sport, with an emphasis on the slow, exacting compulsory figures. In fact, before Sonja, figure skating was just that: the skating of figures. A free skating routine might include moves like the "figure eight." Women figure skaters performed very few jumps, and their spins were usually much slower than they are today.

But Sonja did two things to change all that: She made women's figure skating much more athletic, and she added ballet to the free skating, which made it much more pleasing to watch. She also was one of

the first women to wear a short skirt; that made it easier for her to perform more jumps.

By today's standards, Sonja's skating programs were technically very simple, but in her time they were positively radical. Sonja was a

A natural performer, Sonja loved to ham it up and dazzle her audience.

natural ham, a real performer who wanted to dazzle audiences. She was a small woman—5'2", with a huge smile and

THE BETTMAN ARCHIVES

9

bright eyes. When she skated, people fell in love with her—and with figure skating.

Sonja was born on April 8, 1912, in Oslo, Norway. She was the youngest of the two Henie children; she had an older brother, Leif. Her father, Wilhelm Henie, was a wealthy fur merchant and a former competitive cyclist. In 1893, long before Sonja was born, Mr. Henie won the world amateur cycling championship in Antwerp, Belgium. He passed on his competitive spirit to his daughter.

When Sonja was 7 years old, her father gave her figure skates and signed her up for skating lessons. She had already studied ballet for a year, and she took gracefully to the ice. By the next year, she was the children's champion of Oslo. A year later, she was the Norwegian juniors champion. Sonja loved figure skating and was so talented at it that by the time she was 11 years old, she and her parents decided it would be best for her to leave school and continue her education with private tutors. That way, she would have more time to devote to her skating.

At the time, figure skating was very much a sport of the rich. Although the first indoor rink using artificial ice had been built in England in 1875, they were still rare. Most rinks were on frozen ponds, and skaters often had to travel to winter resorts to practice their sport (like skiers do today). When the ice melted in Norway, Sonja would travel to Austria or the Swiss Alps with her mother, who was her constant companion, to continue training. Together, Sonja and her mother roamed around Europe so Sonja could study dance or figure skating with many different coaches.

In 1924, Sonja entered her first Olympic competition, in Chamonix, France. She was only 11 years old, and she had entered the competition mostly for the experience. When she stepped out onto the outdoor rink, she was dressed in a short, fur-trimmed outfit. Most of the women wore mid-calf-length skirts back then, but Sonja wore a knee-length skirt because she was still a child.

With the freedom of her outfit, Sonja could perform moves that had been attempted before only by men. In her free skating program, for example, Sonja did a jump into a sit spin—much to the shock of her critics, who thought this move was not ladylike. Nonetheless, the judges awarded Sonja third place in the free skating. But because she had fared poorly in the compulsory figures competition, which then counted for 60 percent of the total score, Sonja finished last.

Sonja hated to lose. Her Olympic finish inspired her to work even harder. She worked on her compulsory figures until she could execute them with perfection.

Her skating became almost flawless. In 1926, she placed second at the world figure skating championships. She would never lose again. In 1927, she won the first of what would be 10 consecutive world championships.

Sonja was always looking to try new things to make her sport more entertaining. The same year as she won her first world championship, Sonja attended a performance by the great Russian ballerina, Anna Pavlova, that made a big impression on her and revived the interest in ballet she had had as a child. With the help of Tamara Karsavina, a Russian ballerina who taught in London, Sonja became one of the first skaters to adopt ballet moves and choreography into her skating routines.

In 1928, at the Winter Olympics in St. Moritz, Switzerland, 15-year-old Sonja wowed the judges and the audience with her new style of skating, which featured jumps and ballet moves along with Sonja's own beaming personality and flashy skating outfits. She easily won the gold medal, and set off a fashion trend. Other women skaters began to skate in knee-length skirts and beige skating boots like Sonja's (they had usually worn black before). When everyone began copying her style, Sonja went two steps

Although Sonja's outfits and spins seem old-fashioned today, in her time they were considered radical.

PICTURES INC./LIFE MAGAZINE © TIME WARNER INC.

further, turning to white boots— which nearly all women figure skaters wear today—and shorter skirts. The women also copied her style of skating— using dance moves, graceful jumps, and thrilling spins, as they still do today.

By the start of the 1932 Olympics in Lake Placid, New York, Sonja was world-famous. Tickets for the Olympic figure skating competition that year sold out quickly, and Sonja gave a performance that everyone would always remember. She skated onto the ice wearing a white satin outfit trimmed with sparkling rhinestones and a rhinestone-covered hat. Sonja skated with great confidence, performing jumps, spread eagles, and sit spins. As she concluded her routine with a backward sweep down the ice, she was greeted by thunderous applause. She had won her second Olympic gold medal.

By the 1936 Olympics, Sonja had won another four European championships and four more world titles, giving her nine world championships in a row. She was beginning to tire of competitive skating because there was no other woman in the world who could really compete with her. Shortly before the Olympics began, a columnist for *The New York Sun* wrote of her: "No girl has so far equaled Miss Henie's deft artistry. . . . Despite her dainty lines, she has unusual muscular agility and flawless coordination. . . . Her personality gets across to the judges, and if you think that feminine charm doesn't count with masculine officials, you don't know human nature. . . . In Miss Henie's every posture you note that dash of arrogance, beneath a veil of studied shyness, which marks the great artist."

Sonja planned to win the 1936 Olympic gold medal and one more world championship. Then she would retire. Her dream was to be a movie star.

The 1936 Winter Olympics were held in Garmisch-Partenkirchen [*GARmish PAR-ten-keer-chen*], a town in Germany. World War II (which began in 1939) was only three years away, and Adolf Hitler was Germany's leader at the time. The '36 Olympics were to be a showcase for German—and Hitler's—power. Sonja was not one to worry about politics, however; she was more concerned about a young girl named Cecilia Colledge, who was the British champion.

Sonja always liked to build a big lead in the compulsories so she could relax and feel creative during her free skating routine. But after the Olympic compulsory competition, she held just a narrow lead over Cecilia. Sonja, who was too cocky to think that perhaps she had performed poorly, was so upset with the judges' scoring that she asked her coach and family to tear down the posted scores. Of course, they wouldn't. In a display of bad sportsmanship, Sonja tore them down herself.

She needn't have worried. In the free skating routine, Cecilia skated second of 26 skaters, and she fell. Sonja skated last, with all the pressure gone. It was just growing dark at the open-air skating rink, and a spotlight was turned on. With Hitler sitting in the audience, Sonja skated into the spotlight and performed like a star. Her performance was described by *The New York Times* as a "brilliant execution of spins, twirls and jumps."

A week later, in late February of 1936, Sonja won her 10th world championship, and then retired. In the beginning of March, she and her father sailed to the United States, where she announced that she was becoming a professional skater and would perform in one of the newly created ice shows. Sonja had signed a contract worth at least $70,000 to skate in a 10-city U.S. tour. "I want to go into pictures," Sonja told reporters upon turning pro, "and I want to skate in them. I want to do with skates what Fred Astaire is doing with dancing." Fred Astaire was an American actor and dancer who starred in many movies.

It wasn't long before Sonja got her wish. Her ice shows were so popular that she was able to sign a lucrative movie deal. After watching Sonja perform in a Hollywood exhibition, Darryl F. Zanuck, the head of 20th Century Fox, offered her $10,000 to make a film. But Sonja, a shrewd businesswoman, reportedly demanded 10 times that—and got it.

Sonja's first American film, *One in a Million*, was almost a biography of her life, a story of a young skater's rise to Olympic glory. The film was a box-office hit, as was her next film, *Thin Ice*. The films showed American audiences figure skating as they had never seen it before, with Sonja Henie's artistry. (No one had been able to watch her skate in the Olympics on television. Although television had been invented in 1929, telecasts were few, and live telecasts from Europe weren't possible until 1965.) Ice skating became more popular as a result, and Sonja became richer.

In 1937, Sonja made more than $200,000 from

her movies alone. Sportswriters, not usually taken with women athletes, wrote that Sonja was "the greatest box-office draw in the history of sport." Sonja also continued starring in ice shows, but now she owned and managed her own. It was called "Sonja Henie's Hollywood Ice Revue." By 1940 she was a millionaire.

Away from the screen and the rink, though, Sonja's life progressed less smoothly. In 1937, her father, who had always been her inspiration, died. In 1940, she married Dan Topping, a New York millionaire sportsman and socialite, and soon afterward became a U.S. citizen. Sonja and Dan seemed like a perfect match, but the marriage ended six years later. Sonja married again, in 1949, to Winthrop Gardiner, Jr., another socialite sportsman. That marriage failed, too; Sonja and Winthrop were divorced in 1956.

By that time, Sonja was all but retired. In 1952, her ice show had suffered a tragedy. On the show's opening night in Baltimore, Maryland, a section of the bleachers collapsed and injured 277 spectators. The show was canceled, and nearly $6 million in lawsuits were filed. Even though Sonja still loved to perform, she appeared only occasionally after that, usually in television specials.

Shortly after her second divorce, Sonja married Niels Onstad, a Norwegian shipping executive whom she had known since she was a child. Finally, Sonja found happiness. Sonja and Niels lived in both Los Angeles and Norway. When she and Niels were in Los Angeles, she frequently rose at 7 a.m. to skate at a nearby public rink. She never lost her love of skating.

On October 12, 1969, at the age of 57, Sonja died of leukemia, which is a kind of cancer of the blood. At the time of her death, she was flying from Paris to Oslo with her husband, for emergency treatment of her illness.

Sonja left behind skating records and accomplishments that will probably never be matched. No woman singles skater yet has equaled her 3 Olympic gold medals and 10 consecutive world championships.

PICTURES INC./LIFE MAGAZINE © TIME WARNER INC.

After winning 10 straight world titles and 3 gold medals, Sonja retired to skate in ice shows and the movies.

Eight years after her death, Dick Button, a former Olympic figure skating champion and currently a commentator for ABC Sports, was asked to name the greatest woman skater in history. "If I had to name one," he said, "it would have to be Sonja Henie. She had the most distinguished competitive career, and she clearly affected the sport more than anyone before or after."

Carlo Fassi, who coached Peggy Fleming and Dorothy Hamill, summed up Sonja's influence even more strongly. "Henie," he said, "was the first one to bring skating to the world."

CHAPTER 2

Dick Button

The father of athletic skating was the first American to outskate the world

ANTHONY LINCK/LIFE MAGAZINE © TIME WARNER INC.

Dick Button was the father of the "American style" of men's figure skating—an aggressive and athletic approach to the sport. He was also the first American man to win figure skating's highest honors.

In 1948, Dick won the European figure skating championship, the Olympic gold medal in figure skating, and the world figure skating championship. As if that weren't enough, he also won the U.S. and North American championships, giving him the "grand slam" of figure skating.

He won each competition in his typical style: by skating a daring and nearly flawless program, which thrilled audiences and drew high scores from judges.

The people of the United States were so proud of the man who had become the first American skater to win a gold medal at the Olympics that when Dick arrived home, he was greeted by the celebration of "Dick Button Day" in his hometown of Englewood, New Jersey, complete with a parade and a banquet in his honor. Because of World War II, the Olympics were not held in 1940 or 1944, so it had

been a long time since America had been able to cheer for its Olympic heroes.

Before the war, European skaters had dominated all world and Olympic competitions. But during the war, most of the major skating competitions had to be canceled. In Europe many of the skating coaches, teachers, and skaters were involved in the war effort. Others came to the U.S. during these years. Because of the bombing of so many European cities, those skaters who wanted to skate had no place to practice. As a result, when the war ended, American skaters like Dick Button got their chance to shine.

Dick was born on July 18, 1929, to George and Evelyn Button in Englewood, a suburb of New York City. Mr. Button was president of the Wholesale Typewriter Company, a prosperous business located in Manhattan. Dick was the youngest of three children, all brothers; George Jr. was seven years

Dick strived for excellence in his compulsory figures as well as in his free skating programs.

older than Dick, and Jack was three years older.

Dick started skating with hockey skates when he was 5 years old at a lake near his home. When he was 12, he asked his dad for new skates for Christmas. To his dismay, Dick received another pair of hockey skates; he had hoped for figure skates. "I didn't care much for speed skating," Dick said later. "There just doesn't seem too much point to just skating around and around. Figure skating had more variety. That was for me." The Buttons exchanged the skates, and Dick got his first pair of figure skates.

He didn't cut a graceful figure on the ice, though. At 5'2" tall and 160 pounds, young Dick was roly-poly. The teaching pro at the Rivervale (New Jersey) Club, where Dick started to skate, told Mr. Button to forget about Dick ever becoming an accomplished skater.

Dick didn't pay any attention. He loved figure skating and he was sure he could become a champion. Mr. Button took Dick to see Gus Lussi, a famous skating coach in Lake Placid, New York. Mr. Button told Mr. Lussi: "Watch Dick when the boy doesn't know you are around. If Dick has ability, tell me, and we'll hope you can coach him. If he hasn't, I'll encourage the boy to forget skating. Dick worries about it too much."

In 1952, after winning his second Olympic gold medal, Dick celebrated with his father (left) and his coach, Gus Lussi (right).

Mr. Lussi watched Dick, and arrived at his verdict. "The boy has all the natural ability and determination he needs," said Mr. Lussi. "I think we can make a champion out of him."

Mr. Button didn't tell Dick what the coach had said, but he did encourage him to continue. During vacations and summers, Dick went to study under Mr. Lussi in Lake Placid, about 250 miles away. During the school year, he would rise at 5:30 every morning to skate for a few hours before school. After school, he practiced more, and even more on the weekends. He would perfect one move or jump, and then move on to another. He wasn't afraid to try anything.

When he was 14, Dick won the U.S. novice championship. He won the U.S. junior championship at 15, the senior championship at 16, and the North American championship at 18. Dick did more than just win, though. He began to change the sport of figure skating.

At the time, the Europeans did not place much emphasis on skating as an athletic endeavor. The British skaters believed in the absolute mastery of the figures, while the Austrians—particularly those from the capital city of Vienna—sought to use skating as a way to express music. The routines of Gillis Grafstrom of Sweden, who won the 1920, '24, and '28 Olympic gold medals, and Karl Schafer of Austria, who won the '32 and '36 Olympic gold, were both good examples of the Viennese style.

However, under the coaching of Gus Lussi, Dick brought a new athleticism to men's figure skating. He invented jumps, and took existing jumps to greater heights than ever before. He soared through the air, and kept soaring, until people wondered if he hadn't found a way to defy gravity. Dick introduced maneuvers in competition that he and Mr. Lussi had thought up during their practices, including the flying sit spin and the flying camel spin. The flying sit spin was a jump into a sit spin, and the flying camel was a jump into a camel spin.

For the 1948 Olympics in St. Moritz, Switzerland, Dick tried a move that was particularly daring at the time—a double Axel, two and a half turns in the air. Unlike most jumps in figure skating, which begin and end with the skater gliding backward, the Axel begins with the skater facing forward. While most spins involve one 360-degree rotation, in the Axel, the skater must spin an extra half rotation to wind up facing backward. That is what makes the Axel so difficult.

No skater had ever performed a double Axel in competition before, but Dick intended to try. Two days before the free skating competition in St. Moritz, Dick successfully completed a double Axel in practice. He wanted to include the new move in his Olympic program, but he wasn't sure he was ready.

Dick decided to take the risk. He attempted the double Axel during his Olympic free skating program and landed it perfectly. He was awarded first place by eight of the nine Olympic judges and won the gold medal.

Only a week later, Dick was in Davos, Switzerland, to compete in the world championships. He skated brilliantly again. For his free skating program, four of the nine international judges awarded him scores of 5.9 out of a perfect score of 6.0.

Dick's accomplishments were even more remarkable considering that he was a full-time student. In the

fall of 1949, Dick entered Harvard University, near Boston, and majored in political theory. He practiced at the Skating Club of Boston, only a mile and a half from his dorm, for an hour a day. On the weekends, he spent more time at the rink. Harvard allowed him time off from school every year to practice or skate in competition. Whenever he could, he went to Lake Placid to study with Gus Lussi.

The limited time for skating was just fine for Dick. His education came first. "I really think I did it right," Dick said later. "So many kids drop out of school and spend all their time skating and becoming one-dimensional and eventually bring nothing to their skating. Going to school at the same time, I always came to skating with a feeling that I hadn't yet done it, that I hadn't peaked. It is terribly important to peak at the right time, not to get exhausted or bored."

The most acrobatic skater the sport had ever seen, Dick invented new jumps in practice and took old ones to new heights.

Dick continued to peak at all the right times. From the 1948 Olympics to the 1952 Olympics, he was almost unbeatable. After winning his second straight world championship, in Paris, Dick was awarded the 1949 James E. Sullivan Memorial Trophy, given to the top amateur athlete in the U.S. He was the first winter sports athlete ever to receive the award. Dick responded by winning his third world championship in 1950, in London.

By the time the 1952 Olympics began, Dick had won four world championships, six U.S. senior championships, three North American titles, and the 1948 European championship. (Because of Dick's dominance in the European championship, Americans are no longer eligible to compete in that annual event.) He was the overwhelming favorite to win his second Olympic gold medal.

The 1952 Olympics were held in Oslo, Norway. Just as he had at the 1948 Olympics, Dick wanted to introduce a new move during the competition: the triple loop, a jump with three full turns in the air. The loop was the simplest of all triple jumps because the skater takes off and lands on the same edge of the same skate, but no skater had ever landed any triple jump in competition.

Dick had done the triple loop many times in practice. At the Olympics, he didn't even need the triple jump to win. He had already built a strong lead in the compulsory competition. But Dick wanted to push the sport to its limits.

When the time arrived to perform the triple loop in his free skating routine, though, Dick became nervous and wasn't so sure he could do it. "I forgot in a momentary panic which shoulder should go forward and which back," he wrote later in his autobiography, *Dick Button on Skates.* "I was extraordinarily conscious of the judges, who looked so immobile at rinkside. But this was it. . . . The wind cut my eyes, and the coldness caused tears to stream down my cheeks. Up! Up! Height was vital. Round

and around again in a spin which took only a fraction of a second to complete before it landed on a clean steady back edge. I pulled away breathless, excited and overjoyed." The judges were overjoyed, as well. All nine placed Dick first, and he won his second gold medal.

One week later, Dick was in Paris to try for his fifth consecutive world championship. He won the competition easily. When he returned to the United States, he signed a contract worth $150,000 with the 1953 Ice Capades to make limited appearances in their shows. Dick had been admitted to Harvard Law School, and he only wanted to skate during school breaks.

After 13 weeks of trying to skate and attend law school, though, Dick became very ill with both mononucleosis, a virus that causes symptoms similar to the flu, and hepatitis, an inflammation of the liver. He had to choose between ice shows and school—and he chose school. After graduating from law school, Dick formed his own company, which produced television shows, including *Superstars* and *Battle of the Network Stars,* and invested in plays, such as *A Little Night Music* in London and *Same Time Next Year* on Broadway.

In 1962, Dick began another successful career, this time as a skating commentator for ABC Sports. When people watch figure skating competitions now, they are usually guided by Dick's expert commentary. Dick's figure skating broadcasts are so good that he received an Emmy Award for them in 1981.

It's no surprise that Dick is thorough in his sports reporting. He always strived for excellence in everything he did, particularly skating. "Skating is not like track where an athlete shaves off a tenth of a second to set a new record," Dick told the *Los Angeles Times* in 1976. "My definition of greatness in skating is someone who reaches the top, and leaves the sport different and better because he was in it."

By his own definition, then, Dick Button was one of skating's true greats.

CHAPTER 3

Tenley Albright

Dedication made her the first American woman to capture the gold

When Tenley Albright was 6 years old, in 1941, she came to her first grade teacher with a problem. Tenley was upset, and her teacher asked what was wrong.

Tenley said that she had made a mistake: She had forgotten to capitalize the *A* in Albright on a worksheet she had just handed in. The teacher said not to worry; Tenley could just throw the paper away and begin again.

"No," Tenley responded. "It's wartime."

The United States was beginning to fight in World War II, and basics such as paper were in short supply. The teacher suggested that Tenley turn her paper over and redo the work on the back. "Then the mistake will be on the other side," Tenley replied. Finally, the teacher told Tenley to erase the error. Tenley did, but said, "I still made the mistake."

Even at a young age, Tenley Albright was a perfectionist. She had boundless energy, never gave up, and always worked at something until she got it right. Those traits would eventually help her in 1956 to become the first American woman to win an Olympic gold medal in figure skating.

Tenley was born in Boston, Massachusetts, on

Tenley's seemingly effortless moves came as a result of hours of practice.

PETER STACKPOLE/LIFE MAGAZINE © TIME WARNER INC.

July 18, 1935, to a wealthy surgeon, Hollis Albright, and his wife, Elin. The family, which included Tenley's younger brother, Niles, lived in a large, elegant house in Newton Centre, a Boston suburb. While Tenley was close to both of her parents, she particularly admired her father. Early in her life, she decided that she wanted to be a doctor, just like him.

When Tenley was 8, she was given a pair of skates for Christmas. She loved gliding around in them. The next year, her father flooded an area in the family's backyard to make a rink for her. She also began lessons at the Skating Club of Boston, one of the oldest and most famous skating clubs in the country.

Maribel Vinson, a nine-time U.S. champion, worked as a coach at the Skating Club. When Ms. Vinson first saw Tenley skate, she thought she showed great promise for a 10-year-old. But the coach was concerned that Tenley, like so many children, had no interest in practicing her compulsory figures.

One day, Ms. Vinson lectured the Skating Club's young students on the importance of practicing figures. Without putting in long hours of figures practice, the coach said, the skaters could never expect to become champions. Most children hated compulsories because executing the figures was a slow and boring task.

But two weeks after that lecture, Tenley approached the coach. "I'd just like to tell you, Miss Vinson, that you are absolutely right about the school figures," Tenley said. "I began to practice them, and they're just fascinating."

Just as Tenley was beginning to progress in her figures, however, she was stricken by a terrible disease called polio. Polio is a virus that causes muscles to weaken and can cause permanent paralysis. Tenley became ill in September of 1946, when she was 11. Her case was not too severe, so she wasn't paralyzed, but she still had to spend three weeks in the hospital. When she left, the muscles around her lower back were seriously weakened.

By November, though, Tenley was back on the ice. Her father and other doctors thought that the exercise would help her recover. "She was very determined," said Willie Frick, the Skating Club's head instructor. "She'd fall, get up, and go right on." Many years later, Maribel Vinson wrote in *Sports Illustrated* that she thought that the determination Tenley showed in conquering polio "may have had a great deal to do with making her a champion."

By overcoming polio, Tenley showed she could overcome almost anything. In January of 1947, four months after her polio attack, she traveled to Philadelphia to enter the eastern juvenile skating competition, which is held for skaters under the age of 13. She won. From then on, Tenley began to win one competition after another. When she was 14, in 1950, she won the national junior figure skating championship. In 1951, she competed against skaters of all ages to win the women's senior eastern championship; she came in second at the nationals. These titles qualified her to compete in the 1952 Olympics in Oslo, Norway.

Tenley was an unknown in international figure skating circles back then. She had not even become the U.S. national champion yet, so she didn't expect to do very well at the Olympics. But Tenley surprised herself—and the rest of the world. She won a silver medal! Jeanette Altwegg, an experienced skater from Great Britain, won the women's gold medal. A month later, Tenley competed in the U.S. championships, and this time she won. It was the first of five consecutive national championships she would win.

Tenley's skating style was, as you might expect, one of perfection. She always performed well in compulsory figures. She also skated beautifully in the free skating program. She tried difficult jumps, such as double loops and double Salchows, but only after she had perfected them through hours of prac-

Although her style was slow and graceful, Tenley did not skimp on difficult jumps, spins, and leaps.

PETER STACKPOLE/LIFE MAGAZINE © TIME WARNER INC.

tice. She left nothing to chance.

At 5'6", Tenley was tall, slender, and quite pretty, with blonde hair and bright blue eyes that made her look all-American. Tenley took dance classes along with her skating lessons, so she had the grace of a ballerina. She didn't just skate from jump to jump, but instead allowed the music to dictate her moves. She skated with a slower, more balletic style than that which we see today.

Don't get the idea, however, that Tenley skimped on the athletic aspects of skating. Her leaps were high, and her spins were very fast. Most of all, her style was "clean." Every movement was clearly defined.

In 1953, Tenley's skating style won the approval of the judges at the world figure skating championships, which no American woman had won before. The championships were held that year in Davos, Switzerland. Tenley had built a strong lead in the compulsory competition and then performed her free skating routine on an open-air rink in subzero temperatures that caused some skaters to faint. *The New York Times* wrote: "So difficult were the free skating figures which Miss Albright selected and so brilliant was her execution that all seven judges placed her first." Tenley became the first American woman ever to win the world championship.

Many people thought that after becoming world champion Tenley might want to become a professional skater. But she had no interest in ice shows. "I love skating for skating," Tenley said. "I want to continue as an amateur."

What Tenley really wanted to do was to become a doctor. In the fall of 1953, she entered Radcliffe College, a women's school that is now part of Harvard University. When she wasn't attending classes, she practiced her skating for three to six hours a day.

The next year, Tenley returned to the world championships in Oslo, Norway, to defend her title. She was favored to win. She built up a safe lead in the compulsories over Gundi Busch, a German skater, and was ready to win her second world championship. During Tenley's free skating program, though, she leapt into a combination Axel

and double loop jump and fell flat on the ice. She was stunned, but she got up and finished the rest of her program.

Gundi Busch won the championship, and Tenley felt awful. Soon afterward, Tenley went to another rink and practiced the combination until she got it right. "Right then," she said, "I had to go off by myself and do that jump again and again to prove that I could do it without falling."

No woman had ever lost the world championship and regained it, but Tenley was determined to become the first. She returned to the championships in 1955, in Vienna this time, and won back her world crown. Then she had only one goal left: the Olympic gold medal.

Tenley decided to take off the fall 1955 semester from Radcliffe to train for the 1956 Olympics in Cortina, Italy. The summer before, she took the classes she would need so that she wouldn't be behind after the Olympics. But Tenley hadn't slacked off on her training.

On a typical summer day, the energetic 19-year-old arose at 4:00 a.m., skated for several hours, sped to Radcliffe for classes (in the Porsche her father had given her), then went back to skating. In the evening, she skated again and studied.

Tenley arrived in Italy early for the Olympics, in order to practice and adjust to the rink. However, two weeks before the competition, she was skating backwards at the Olympic rink when she struck a hole in the ice. As she fell, the edge of the blade on her left skate cut through her right boot, severing a vein and scraping a bone. It was a very bad cut, and although it did not require stitches, it seriously weakened her ankle. The U.S. team doctor patched it up, and two days later Tenley's dad arrived to look after the wound. Tenley was able to practice her skating for barely an hour a day after that, and she avoided jumps in which she landed on her right foot.

Tenley was worried. She wanted the gold medal badly, but so did her rival, a 16-year-old American named Carol Heiss. Carol had skated against Tenley many times, and although she had always lost, their scores were frequently very close. But this time, Carol felt she could beat her, especially with Tenley's bad ankle.

When the skating competition began, Tenley won the compulsory figures, but only by a slight margin over Carol. That meant that in the free skating program, the two would be battling to see who would become the first American woman to win an Olympic figure skating gold medal.

On the final day of competition, the sun shone brightly when Tenley stepped onto the outdoor rink to begin her free skating routine. She was wearing a dark rose sweater and red flowers in her hair, and a large bandage that ran from her right ankle up to near her calf. Her parents stood on the sideline, and her father watched nervously, holding his breath each time Tenley did a jump and landed on her right foot.

Tenley skated to the music of Jacques Offenbach, a 19th-century French composer, and she moved as if her ankle injury had never happened. She whirled through a complicated routine of Axels, split jumps, and cross foot spins. Only once did her bad ankle seem to buckle, but she regained her balance quickly. Even though she hadn't been able to practice much since her injury, all the hours of practice she had put in over the years were now paying off.

As Tenley limped off the ice after she had finished, she finally let herself admit how difficult these Olympics had been for her. "It is all over now, and I can say that my leg has not stopped hurting once since I cut it two weeks ago," she confessed to reporters. Even

so, Tenley received a first place vote from 10 of the 11 judges, and won the gold medal.

Carol got her win a few days later by beating Tenley at the world championships. But Tenley turned right around a few weeks after that and beat Carol for the U.S. championship. It was the eighth time in nine meetings that Tenley had defeated Carol.

Tenley's attention soon turned elsewhere. In 1957, she entered Harvard's medical school, and in 1961, she became a surgeon. She went into practice with her father.

In 1962, Tenley married Tudor Gardiner, a prominent Bostonian, and they had three daughters. But her marriage didn't last, and she married for a second time, to Gerald Blakeley. Tenley continued her work as surgeon until only recently, skating whenever she could, and staying involved in the sport. She has served on the United States Olympic committee and on the International Olympic Committee.

Tenley Albright was a rare woman for her time: a sports champion and, later, a successful surgeon. Everything Tenley did, she did well. She would accept nothing less than perfection from herself.

THE BETTMAN ARCHIVES

Following her gold medal performance, Tenley retired to become a doctor.

CHAPTER 4

David and Hayes Jenkins

Brotherly love—and rivalry—made them the only siblings to win Olympic gold

Hayes Alan Jenkins, 22, had just finished skating his long program at the 1956 Winter Olympics in Cortina, Italy. The outdoor rink had been hard and bumpy, but that hadn't stopped Hayes from skating the long, smooth strokes that were his trademark. His Cortina program had many jumps, including a double Axel and a double Lutz—both of which he had executed perfectly.

Hayes, a native of Akron, Ohio, was the 1955 American and world figure skating champion, and all he wanted now was to win an Olympic gold medal. He had won the Olympic compulsories competition, only three days before, by 12 points. But Ronnie Robertson, an 18-year-old Californian, was

in second place after the compulsory figures. If Ronnie skated brilliantly in the long program, he would have a chance to take the gold. Ronnie was a showman; he loved to thrill audiences with daredevil jumps and spins, and he didn't disappoint in Cortina. He kept the spectators on the edge of their seats as he performed a triple loop and a triple Salchow. Only two other men had ever tried a triple Salchow in competition.

After both Hayes and Ronnie had skated, the waiting began. The judges couldn't decide who should be awarded first place. Wrapped in fur coats, the judges huddled on the edge of the ice.

Scoring a skater's performance is a very complicated procedure. After awarding scores to all of the skaters, the judges hand the scores to an accountant,

THE BETTMAN ARCHIVES

Hayes was a classical skater, who preferred smooth footwork and good musical timing to acrobatic leaps.

who tallies them up. If a judge gives a skater the best score, then that skater receives one point for a first-place finish. A skater who is considered second-best by a judge receives two points, and so on. After all the judges' scores are added up, the skater with the lowest number of points is the winner.

In this case, however, several judges had scored Hayes and Ronnie equally, so the judges had to go through an even more complicated method of tiebreaking. Hayes and his family, who had watched from the stands, were growing restless. Finally, unable to bear the strain, David, Hayes's 19-year-old brother, who had also skated in the event, turned to Hayes and said, "If they take this one away from you, I'll never skate again!"

When the judges finally finished, they declared Hayes the winner by less than one point. In all his worry over his brother, David had ignored his own success. He had won the bronze medal. It was the first time all three medals had gone to Americans.

Fortunately, David didn't quit skating. After Hayes retired to go to Harvard Law School, David kept the U.S. and world championship in the family. At the 1960 Winter Olympics, David also won an Olympic gold medal. The Jenkins are the only siblings to have each won gold medals in the Olympic singles figure skating competition.

Skating ability ran in the Jenkins family like blue eyes or good looks runs in other families. Even Hayes's and David's older sister, Nancy, was a skater. It wasn't as if their parents were accomplished skaters, though. Hayes R. Jenkins, their father, was a corporate lawyer at a tire company in Akron. Their mother, Sara, enrolled the children in skating lessons when they were young, but not because she wanted them to become Olympic champions. She put them in lessons at the Cleveland Skating Club on Saturday mornings because that was when she liked to clean. She wanted the children out of the house!

Ms. Jenkins had her clean house—and her boys became champions. In 1948, just before his 15th birthday, Hayes won the midwestern senior men's championship. Nine days after his birthday, he won the national juniors championship.

As Hayes began to compete among the men at national and international competitions, he found himself in the shadow of the great American skater Dick Button, who held the U.S. championship from 1946 through 1952 and the world title from 1948 through 1952. For a time, Hayes even considered quitting because he thought he'd never have a chance to become champion. "I got quite used to the back seat," Hayes said later. "But I thought it would be stupid not to try for what I have been working for all my life."

In 1951, Hayes left home to go to Northwestern University in Evanston, Illinois, a suburb of Chicago. But he had a long commute from school to the nearest skating rink. So, when Colorado College in Colorado Springs offered him a scholarship, Hayes decided to transfer to the other school. There, he could also work with Edi Scholdan, a famous skating coach. Soon afterward, Hayes's father arranged a job transfer, and the entire Jenkins family joined Hayes in Colorado Springs so that David could work with Mr. Scholdan too.

Hayes skated well enough in the 1951 U.S. championships to qualify to compete in the 1952 Winter Olympics in Oslo, Norway. Of course, the unbeatable Dick Button won the gold medal. But Hayes finished a respectable fourth, behind Helmut

Seibt of Austria and Jim Grogan of the United States. Finally, after winning the 1952 world championship, Dick Button announced his retirement. Helmut Seibt also left competitive skating. Hayes finally would have his chance to be No. 1.

In March of 1953, Hayes went to Davos, Switzerland, to compete in the world championships. Although Jim Grogan was favored to win, Hayes, now seasoned by age and experience, skated beautifully. He won the first of what would be his four consecutive world championships.

Now, it was Hayes's turn to cast *his* shadow over another skater— his brother, David. In 1953, David won the men's midwestern championship. He then went to the U.S. championships, and won the national junior title. Hayes, who was competing at the senior level, won the U.S. men's championship.

After that, Hayes and David would compete against one another often, but they were always each other's strongest supporter. They trained under the same coach, went to the same college, and always cheered for the other to do well. That may have been because, even though they were brothers, they were very different skaters.

At six feet, Hayes was six inches taller than David. Long-limbed Hayes skated in a classical, almost rigid manner. He didn't believe in trying new tricks and jumps; he thought that good skating—that is, good footwork, a sense of the music, etc.—should speak for itself. Hayes wasn't as creative as Dick Button or his brother, but he had great control of his body and was a very beautiful skater. He believed in technical mastery of figure skating, and he arrived at it through endless hours of practice.

David, at 5'6", was a more compact skater. He used his tremendous leg strength to leap high into the air, and dazzled audiences with jumps and spins. David was more athletic and willing to try new things. Dick Button may have introduced the triple jump, but David, along with Ronnie Robertson, was one of the first men to regularly include a variety of triple jumps in his routine.

When Hayes and David skated against each other, Hayes always won. In 1954, when Hayes won

the U.S. championships, David finished right behind him. At the world championships, Hayes was first, and David came in fourth. At the 1955 world championships in Vienna, Austria, Hayes placed first, Ronnie Robertson second, and David third. The trio finished in that order again at the 1956 Olympics, at the 1956 worlds, and at the U.S. championships in Philadelphia. When Hayes left competitive skating after that year, he predicted that his little brother would become the next world champion, and he was right. Of course, it didn't hurt David that Ronnie Robertson had decided to turn professional.

In March of 1957, David won his first world championship, which was held that year right in Colorado Springs. *The New York Times* described David as "executing daring spins and leaps that no one else attempted." *Time* magazine wrote, "Jenkins seemed to spend as much time soaring in the air as on the ice." Later that month, David won the U.S. championship in Berkeley, California. From then on, he was all but unbeatable. He won the U.S. and world championships for the next three years—but not for a lack of competition.

At the 1959 world championships in Colorado Springs, David's reign was threatened by an 18-year-old Canadian named Donald Jackson. Don was the

David was an athletic skater, and one of the first to include a variety of triple jumps in his routine.

Canadian and North American champion, and a spectacular free skater; he later became the first man to land a triple Lutz in competition.

At the 1959 world championships, Donald skated before David, and performed so well that David knew he would have to dazzle the judges to keep his title. Dazzle them he did. "He whirled through spectacular jumps and spins in such a fluid manner that the program was pure musical artistry," said *The New York Times* of David's performance.

David kept his world title, and now he could focus on a loftier goal: winning a gold medal at the 1960 Olympics. He didn't have much time to practice during the school year, though, because he was already in medical school at Case Western Reserve University in Cleveland.

David spent the summer before the Olympics in Colorado Springs, training with Edi Scholdan. But in late August, just as he was preparing to return to medical school, David had a freak accident. During a practice, he collided with another skater, Gregory Kelly, and the blade of Gregory's skate gashed David's right leg and cut his calf muscle. The injury required 30 stitches, and David was forced to wear a cast to support the muscle while it healed.

By February, when the Olympics were held in Squaw Valley, California, David's leg was fine. Never one to waste a moment, he had even brought 34 pounds of medical schoolbooks with him to Squaw Valley, thinking he might have a chance to study. But he didn't crack the books once. "I was too busy worrying," he said later. There was plenty to worry about. When the figure skating competition began, a Czechoslovakian named Karol Divin won the compulsories. David knew he had to skate perfectly in the free skating program to beat Karol—and Donald Jackson, who was always a threat.

In his long program, David skated to the music of Edvard Grieg, a 19th century Norwegian composer.

At first, David eased into the music, but then he dramatically displayed his great athletic ability. He exploded into a combination of two double Axel jumps, a triple Salchow, and then a flying camel spin that sent the more than 8,000 spectators into a roar of applause. The routine was so thrilling and flawlessly executed that it caused Sonja Henie, the three-time Olympic champion who watched the performance, to exclaim, "He's wonderful!"

The judges agreed. One of them was so carried away by David's performance that he broke into applause at the end—something that skating judges are never, ever supposed to do. David received one score of 5.8, seven 5.9's and one rare 6.0, a perfect score. Although Donald Jackson skated well, he could not top these scores. David won the gold, Karol won the silver, and Don, the bronze. "Dave was great—just magnificent," Don said after the competition was over. "He deserved to win. Nobody could touch him today."

Hayes was thrilled that David had won, but he was also thrilled for the women's gold medal winner, Carol Heiss. Carol was the U.S. and world champion, and she was also Hayes's fiancée. That April, Hayes and Carol were married, increasing the family total to three gold medals. Hayes and Carol moved to Akron, where Hayes practiced law and Carol became a skating coach. David went on to become a doctor.

Hayes and David Jenkins dominated figure skating from 1953 to 1960. Between them, they won eight U.S. and eight world championships. But they never lost sight of what was really important: their friendship as brothers. Even after David won his gold medal, he continued to heap praise upon his brother. "When Hayes won, that was the biggest thrill of my life, even bigger than when I won here," David said at the 1960 Olympics. "My brother is the greatest skater I ever saw."

CHAPTER 5

Carol Heiss

After so many silver medals, she promised her dying mother a gold—and delivered

When Carol Heiss was 16, she made a promise to her mother. Carol had just won the silver medal at the 1956 Olympics, but her mother, who was dying of cancer, was disappointed that her daughter hadn't won the gold. Carol promised that at the next Olympics she would win the gold medal. Carol's mother died that fall. Four years later, true to her word, Carol became the Olympic champion.

Carol's skating career was often guided by her mother's wishes. Marie Heiss was a strong, domineering woman who was very involved in her children's lives. Both she and her husband, Edward, had emigrated from Germany. They lived in Ozone Park, Queens, in New York City, where Mr. Heiss worked in a bakery, decorating cakes.

Carol was born on January 30, 1940. Her sister, Nancy, was born two years later and her brother, Bruce, two years after that. They were high-spirited and

Carol's mother, Marie Heiss, pushed and sacrificed to help Carol reach the top.

mischievous children, and Marie Heiss decided that they needed to burn off their energy in sports. So, when Carol was 5, her mother took her ice skating.

Carol was a natural and graceful skater. Within a year, Carol was taking lessons at the New York Figure Skating Club in Manhattan. The club's coaches were Andrée and Pierre Brunet, a French couple who had won the Olympic pairs skating gold medal in 1928 and 1932.

Pierre told Marie Heiss that Carol could become a figure skating champion in 10 years if she was willing to skate seven or eight hours a day, every day. Ms. Heiss decided then that

THE BETTMAN ARCHIVE

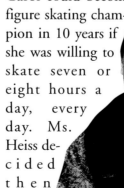

Carol would indeed become a champion, and did everything she could to help her daughter achieve that goal. Ms. Heiss couldn't afford a baby-sitter when she took Carol into Manhattan for skating lessons, so she always took Nancy and Bruce along. They soon became skaters, too, and were quite successful—but not as successful as Carol.

Carol paid a price for her early success. She had to follow a very strict schedule, as Pierre had predicted, leaving her little time for fun or socializing. Every weekday, Marie Heiss would wake her children at 5:30 a.m. They would eat breakfast, and then drive to Manhattan to start skating at 7. Carol skated for about 4 1/2 hours before dashing off to the Professional Children's School, which offered a flexible class schedule. After that, Carol would go home, eat supper, study and fall asleep by 9 p.m. She also practiced on weekends.

The Heisses also made great sacrifices for Carol's career. Edward Heiss did not earn much money at the bakery, so Marie Heiss helped out by working as a free-lance clothing designer. "It's a labor of love," she once said. "Some people buy a new car every year or put money into an expensive home. But our money all goes into the skating fund."

For Marie Heiss, the sacrifices were all worth it, especially as Carol improved. In 1950, Carol won the mid-Atlantic regional and the eastern sectional junior championships. That year, she also teamed with her sister, Nancy, to win the mid-Atlantic similar pairs crown. (Back then, pairs could be of the same sex, although there was also a contest for mixed pairs.) In 1953, when she was 13, Carol came in second to Tenley Albright, who was 4 1/2 years older, at the U.S. senior national championships. That same year, Carol went to her first world championships. Tenley Albright won, but Carol came in fourth.

The next year, Carol decided, would be *her* year to win the worlds. In 1927, Sonja Henie had become world champion at the age of 15, and Carol wanted to better that. But at a practice two weeks before the 1954 competition, Nancy and Carol accidentally collided during a jump. Nancy's skate slashed Carol's Achilles tendon, which is the tendon that joins the calf muscles to the bone in the heel.

The injury was painful and hobbling, and Carol had to miss the worlds. She couldn't practice or compete for several months. But Carol recovered in time to come in second—again behind Tenley—at the U.S. championships in Los Angeles in March.

Carol was still only 15, and skaters usually don't peak until their early 20's. Tenley, however, was already at *her* peak. Both were talented athletes, but while Carol was a more bubbly and energetic skater who always played to the crowds, Tenley was more graceful and her polished style was the one that the judges seemed to like. Carol finished second to Tenley in the 1955 national championships in Colorado Springs, Colorado, and again at the world championships in Vienna, Austria.

Now it was time for Carol to put all those second place finishes behind her and focus her energy on winning a gold medal at the 1956 Olympics in Cortina, Italy. Her biggest rival, once again, would be Tenley. In Cortina, Tenley took a slight lead during the compulsory figures and in the free skating, she skated perfectly and was awarded high scores from the judges.

Carol skated after Tenley. She appeared on the outdoor rink wearing an aquamarine dress and black gloves. As she whirled through her routine of spins and jumps, her blonde ponytail whipped out behind her. She also skated perfectly, and, as she left the rink, the crowd cheered "six, six, six," encouraging the judges to award Carol the perfect score of 6.0.

After all the scores were in, Tenley had won the free skating, and the gold medal. Carol had lost by less than two points. She and her mother were extremely disappointed. It was then that Carol promised her mother that she would one day win an Olympic gold medal. "We call Carol 'the bridesmaid,'" Marie Heiss told reporters afterward, "always second to Tenley."

Carol wouldn't be second for long, though. Seventeen days later, Tenley and Carol met in Germany to compete for the world championship. For the first time ever, Carol took a slight lead over

Tenley in the school figures and, with the help of a flawless free skating program, finally beat the Olympic champion. When Carol realized she had won, she turned to her mother and said, with unabashed joy, "Mother! Do you realize it? I am the best skater in the whole world!"

The Heisses' stay in Germany, however, did not go smoothly. Carol and her mother stayed in a hotel apart from the U.S. skating team. The team hotel supposedly had only one bathroom. U.S. officials complained that the Heisses were being snobby. What the officials didn't know was that the Heisses needed privacy: Marie Heiss was dying of cancer.

When Carol and her mother returned to the United States in March, Marie Heiss's cancer had reached an advanced stage. In October, she died.

From then on, Carol, remembering her promise to her mother, prac-

A bubbly and energetic skater, Carol performed jumps and spins that were considered daring at the time.

THE BETTMAN ARCHIVE

THE BETTMAN ARCHIVE

Besides Carol, her sister Nancy (left) and brother Bruce also went on to become successful skaters.

ticed her skating with even greater devotion and soon became unbeatable. Tenley Albright had retired, leaving Carol alone at the top. Carol won every U.S. championship from 1957 to 1960, and every world championship from 1956 to 1960.

While she devoted long hours to figure skating, Carol also began college in 1957, attending New York University. It wasn't easy being a college student and world-class skater, but if the hard work was too much for Carol, she never showed it.

Carol's bubbly personality and knack for winning over audiences made people compare her to Sonja Henie. "Carol is a winsome lass, bright and cheerful, with the wholesomeness of the nice little kid next door," wrote Arthur Daley of *The New York Times* in 1960. "She has none of Sonja's grandeur, but such are the qualities of her appeal that she can win over spectators without it."

Carol, however, could perform jumps that Sonja wouldn't have dreamed of. Carol performed double flips, double loops, and flying spins. She was one of the few women competitors who included a double Axel in their routine. In practice sessions, she even practiced triple jumps. Her skating had also become graceful and polished. Almost everyone expected her to win a gold medal at the 1960 Olympics.

Carol's greatest competition in the United States came from her sister, Nancy. At the 1959 national championship, Nancy finished in second place behind Carol. Nancy had taken time off from Michigan State University to prepare for the Olympics. But a few months before the Olympics, Nancy broke her ankle and had to withdraw.

Carol, unlike her sister, continued with her university studies—much to her coach's dismay. Only a couple of weeks before the Olympics, she was still taking final exams. "We should be practicing most now," Pierre complained to a reporter. "The

Olympics are coming! Exams? Bah!"

Pierre needn't have worried. When 20-year-old Carol arrived in Squaw Valley, California, for the 1960 Winter Olympics, she was ready. She had practiced almost 30 hours a week for many years. Carol was in the lead after the compulsory figures. She knew that as long as she didn't fall or skate badly in the free skating program, she would win the gold medal.

When Carol arrived at the Blyth Arena to perform her free skating routine, the sun was shining brilliantly. "When I saw the sun shining while I was skating," said Carol, "I felt it was a lovely day to win a gold medal." And that's exactly what she did. She skated effortlessly through a tricky routine, which included two whirling leaps in quick succession, from alternate skates. (It's much easier to take two jumps in a row from the same skate.)

Carol's received first place votes from all nine judges, and beat the silver medalist, Sjoukje Dijkstra of Holland, by 65 points. Carol had won her gold medal!

After the awards ceremony, Carol talked to reporters about the promise she had made to her mom, and she couldn't help but be a little sad. "I gave her my promise," Carol said. "I only wish she could be here now."

There was someone else that Carol wished could be with her. His name was Hayes Alan Jenkins, and he had won the men's figure skating gold medal at the 1956 Olympics. His younger brother, David, won the gold medal that year at Squaw Valley. Hayes was Carol's fiancé. The two had become secretly en-gaged in August of 1959, and did not announce it so that Carol could concentrate on preparing for the Olympics. Hayes and Carol had met at skating competitions when Carol was 11 and Hayes was 18. As they grew older, they fell in love. Hayes couldn't come to Squaw Valley because he had just begun to work as a lawyer.

A few weeks after the Olympics, Carol won her fifth world championship. And on April 30, 1960, she married Hayes. That fall, she went to Hollywood to star in the film *Snow White and the Three Stooges*. She told reporters, "In this way I can repay my father for all that he has done for me. He would never accept the money directly, but if I help my brother and sister it will relieve him of some of the expenses."

Now she and Hayes and their three children live in Akron, Ohio, where Carol works as a skating coach. One of her students is Jill Trenary, the 1990 U.S. figure skating champion.

Carol and Hayes Jenkins, the 1956 gold medalist, were married soon after Carol won her gold medal.

NYT PICTURES

CHAPTER 6

Maribel Vinson Owen

She could not win a world title with her skating, but she won one with her coaching

It was February 15, 1961, and Maribel Vinson Owen and her two daughters, Maribel and Laurence [lo-RAHNS] were flying to Prague, Czechoslovakia, for the world figure skating championships. Laurence, 16, had just won the U.S. national and North American championships, and young Maribel, 20, had won the national pairs skating title with her partner Dudley Richards.

The Owens family was full of hope as they boarded Sabena Airlines Flight 548 in New York City, along with 16 other members of the U.S. skating team and their coaches. The team planned to fly from New York to Brussels, Belgium, and then continue on by plane to Prague.

But as the plane made its approach to land at the Brussels airport, something went terribly wrong.

One of the Boeing 707 jet's engines seemed to stop, and the aircraft shook as though the engine was trying to start again. Then, the plane's nose turned up toward the sky. Seconds later, the plane fell and burst into flames.

Everybody on board was killed. It was a tragic blow to figure skating in the United States, one that took years for the sport to get over. Perhaps the greatest loss of all to American skating, though, was that of Maribel Vinson Owen.

Maribel, who was 49 at the time of her death, had had a tremendous influence on American figure skating. She was a nine-time national champion, and later one of the country's finest coaches. Her most famous student was Tenley Albright, who won the Olympic gold medal in 1956. At the time of the air disaster, Maribel considered her younger daugh-

NYT PICTURES

34

Maribel, shown here at the Rockefeller Center rink in New York, was the United States champion nine times.

ter, Laurence, her next champion.

Maribel Vinson (Owen was her married name) was born in 1911. She was the only child of Thomas Vinson, a Boston lawyer, and his wife, Gertrude. Thomas Vinson had once been a skating champion.

Maribel began skating when she was 3 years old at a nearby rink in Cambridge, Massachusetts. She started on inexpensive double-runner skates, which are skates with two blades. Maribel soon graduated to single-bladed skates and, when she was 10, started taking figure skating lessons. "When she was just a little girl," Maribel's mother recalled, "she told me she was going to be a champion. She worked, and she drove herself."

When Maribel was 12, she became the junior national champion. When she was 16, she became the U.S. women's champion, which qualified her to compete in the Olympics. The 1928 Olympics were held in St. Moritz, Switzerland, and Maribel skated in the shadow of Sonja Henie, one of the greatest figure skaters of all time.

It was Maribel's bad luck to have her skating career coincide with Sonja's. Maribel skated at many

NYT PICTURES

Skating in the shadow of Sonja Henie, Maribel never won a world title—except as coach for Tenly Albright.

of the 10 world championships that Sonja won, from 1927 to 1936, and at the three Olympics that Sonja won—1928, 1932, and 1936. At the 1928 Olympics, Maribel came in fourth. At the world championships only a few weeks later, 16-year-old Maribel finished second to Sonja. But that was as close to toppling Sonja as Maribel ever got. "Sonja's routine is not as hard as mine," Maribel once said. "But she never makes a mistake."

The two women had very different styles. Sonja played to the crowd, while Maribel was more of a serious worker on the ice. She practiced long hours and always tried to learn new moves. "As a figure skater, Maribel was one of the best," wrote sportswriter Arthur Daley of *The New York Times* the day after her death. "Maybe she was even better than the best, meaning Sonja Henie. Glamorous Sonja caught the eyes of the judges in a manner that the plainer, more severe looking Maribel never could do."

While Norwegian-born Sonja continued to beat Maribel in international competitions, Maribel was all but unbeatable at home. After the 1928 Olympics, Maribel enrolled at Radcliffe College, in Cambridge. But she continued at the Skating Club of Boston, under her coach Willie Frick, usually from 5 a.m. to 9 a.m. every morning, before her classes started. She drove herself mercilessly, always trying to improve. By the time the 1932 Olympics began, Maribel had already won five national championships.

The 1932 Olympics were held in Lake Placid, New York. Maddeningly, Maribel still wasn't able to beat Sonja, and had to settle for the bronze medal. It was the only Olympic medal she ever won.

Her graduation from Radcliffe in 1933 freed her to concentrate on her skating, but Maribel was too bright to just skate. In the fall of 1934, she joined

NYT PICTURES

The New York Times as a sports reporter, becoming the first woman ever to join the *Times'* sports staff.

Still, Maribel continued to devote many hours to skating practice. She skipped the U.S. competition in 1934 in order to compete in the European championships, which were held at the same time. Sonja Henie, of course, won. Maribel came in fifth.

Maribel returned to compete in the national championships the following year and won back her crown. It was the seventh time she had won the U.S. title. When she arrived in Garmisch-Partenkirchen, Germany, for the 1936 Olympics, Maribel thought that she had a much better chance at winning the gold medal than she had had at the 1928 or 1932 Games. Her biggest competition, she told reporters, would be Sonja, of course, and an English skater named Cecilia Colledge. A reporter for the *New York American* wrote that "Miss Vinson has improved so much in the past year that anything may happen." What happened, though, was just what

Maribel had high hopes for daughters Maribel (left) and Laurence, but all three were killed in a tragic plane crash.

most people expected to happen: Sonja won the gold medal, and Cecilia won the silver. Maribel finished in fifth place.

Although it is hard to imagine today, given the great success American skaters like Tenley Albright, Carol Heiss, Peggy Fleming, Dorothy Hamill, and Debi Thomas have had, no American woman had yet won a world championship or an Olympic gold medal when Maribel was skating. But while Maribel could not win those championships with her skating, she ultimately won those honors through her coaching.

Maribel won her eighth U.S. national title in Chicago in January of 1936. That year, she also won the national pairs event with Boston skater George Hill. It was the sixth time that Maribel had won the national pairs title, either with George or with her first partner, Thornton Coolidge. The next winter, she won her ninth and final U.S. singles championship in Chicago. She and George came in second in the pairs event.

In March of 1937, Maribel announced her retirement from competitive skating. Two months later she turned professional, joining the Ice Carnival as its featured star and director. Because the show would take so much of her time, Maribel resigned from the staff of the *Times,* though she continued to write articles about skating for newspapers and magazines for the rest of her career.

Maribel's professional skating partner in her ice show was Guy Owen, a skater from Ottawa, Canada. They fell in love, and in September of 1938, they were married. Maribel and Guy continued skating professionally together. In 1942, they had their first daughter, also named Maribel, and in 1944, they had a second, Laurence.

Not long after her first daughter was born, Maribel began to work as a coach in California, where the family lived briefly. The marriage didn't last, though. Maribel moved back to Boston with her daughters, and in April of 1949, she divorced Guy Owen. In 1952, Guy died and Maribel became the family's sole breadwinner. She worked as a coach at the Skating Club of Boston. Soon after she began coaching there, Maribel took on her most famous pupil, Tenley Albright.

Tenley was 10 years old when Maribel began coaching her. Under Maribel's guidance, Tenley developed into one of America's finest skaters, a beautiful and graceful athlete. She won the silver medal at the 1952 Olympics, and the next year she became the first American woman to win the world championship. In 1956, she became the first American woman to win an Olympic gold medal.

After her success with Tenley, Maribel didn't rest on her laurels, however. She had another student that she thought could become an Olympic champion—her daughter, Laurence. Through her work with all of her pupils, Maribel continued to dedicate her life to her sport. In 1961, shortly before the fatal air crash, a reporter from *Sports Illustrated* visited Maribel and described her day in this way: "She is up at five or six every day, teaching her girls early in the morning, then leaping from class to class at rinks all over and around Boston. She frequently has no lunch, and several nights a week has perhaps half an hour for dinner before leaving to teach until 11 or 12. She supervises ice shows and community projects, fusses over costumes and prepares her pupils' music—splicing it for them in the relatively free hours between two and four in the morning."

The Owen girls, Maribel and Laurence, were on ice skates as soon as they could walk. Skating was in their blood, and their mother pushed them as hard as she would have pushed any of her students.

Young Maribel lacked the drive her mother had had. "She didn't have that killer instinct," said Henry Lamar, a family friend. It wasn't until she paired up with skater Dudley Richards, the year before she died, that young Maribel began to win.

Laurence was another story. She was a vivacious young woman who was a natural performer on the ice. Like her mother, she was a driven competitor. In 1960, Laurence placed sixth at the Winter Olympics in Squaw Valley, California.

By early 1961, both young Maribel and Laurence had risen to the top of North American figure skating. Maribel teamed with Dudley and won the national pairs competition. Laurence won the North American women's championship four days before she was killed. She was the United States' hope for the 1961 world championship in Prague.

Because of the tragic air crash in 1961, Laurence never got a chance to show what she might have been able to achieve. But there's no doubt in anyone's mind what her mother, Maribel Vinson Owen, had achieved.

"Every great American skater for the past 25 years has been influenced by Maribel," said Judy Lamar, one of Maribel's students, the day after the crash. "She worked with so many and taught so much, so well, that the methods were passed along wherever skaters met. And when they met and competed, there was Maribel, lending a hand to anybody who needed it. Her drive for perfection was deeply instilled in all of us."

CHAPTER 7

Peggy Fleming

A ballerina on the ice, Peggy brought a new kind of grace and beauty to the sport

When Peggy Fleming skated, it seemed as though she were floating above the ice. At 5'4" and 108 pounds, she was a slight, almost frail young woman, who skated with the grace of a ballerina.

But this style was deceiving. Peggy performed very difficult, athletic moves and simply made them *seem* effortless.

Dick Button, the two-time Olympic gold medalist and television commentator, was moved when he watched 17-year-old Peggy win the 1966 world championship in Davos, Switzerland. "She is a delicate lady on ice," Dick said. "With some skaters, there is a lot of fuss and feathers, but nothing is happening. With Peggy, there's no fuss and feathers, and a great deal is happening. She does certain small things which I know from experience are very difficult... but some people can't even realize she's doing them. The only other skater in her class since the war [World War II] has been Tenley Albright."

In the 1960s, when Peggy competed, women's figure skating was moving toward a more athletic style, with more jumps and spins than ever before. But Peggy wasn't interested

> **The greatest compliment paid Peggy was that she could make the most difficult moves look easy.**

in trying new tricks. She wanted to bring out the beauty of the music and the skating. "I primarily represent the ballet approach," she said. "That is, where the

JOHN G. ZIMMERMAN/SPORTS ILLUSTRATED

movements are more graceful and everything blends smoothly as you flow across the ice."

From the first time Peggy tried skating, she was graceful. She was nine years old, and her family was living in Cleveland, Ohio. "We had never been near an ice rink before," said Peggy's older sister, Janice. "It was amazing. Peggy took to skates right off. She didn't wobble or anything."

Peggy was the second of four daughters born to Albert and Doris Fleming. She was born on July 27, 1948 in San Jose, California. Her sister Janice was a year older; Maxine was two years younger, and Cathy, six years younger.

At the time, most champion skaters came from wealthy families who had enough money to afford the sport's high costs; a coach's fee alone could run to thousands of dollars every year. Peggy's father was a pressman, which means that he ran the printing press at a newspaper. He never earned a lot of money, and the Flemings made great sacrifices for Peggy to become a champion skater. Her mother even sewed Peggy's costumes.

Peggy's father encouraged her skating from the beginning. "He thought I had some potential," Peggy said. "It was his ambition for me to become world champion." Shortly after Peggy started skating, her father took a job with the *Los Angeles Times,* and the family moved to Pasadena. Peggy began to practice and take lessons at a public rink. In 1960, when she was 11, she won the Pacific Coast juvenile championship. The next year, she won the novice championship.

Peggy soon broke into national figure skating circles. When she was 14, in 1963, she won the Pacific Coast *women's* championship, and placed third in the junior nationals. None of those triumphs, however, could prepare the skating world for what Peggy would achieve in 1964. That year, at age 15, Peggy won the United States figure skating championship. The national championships were held in Cleveland, at the arena where Peggy first tried skating. Peggy's free skating program was so graceful and effortless that it drew the first place vote of three of the five judges.

"She went through her program and ended with a fast spin, flawlessly," according to the report in *The New York Times.* "Bystanders were amazed at the brilliance of Miss Fleming's skating and as she continued, she gained confidence and assurance." Peggy had become the youngest U.S. national women's champion ever!

From that day, people began to look to Peggy as the hope of American skating. The Americans were rebuilding their figure skating team, which had suffered a terrible loss in February of 1961, when the entire U.S. skating team was killed in a plane crash on the way to Prague, Czechoslovakia. For the 12 years before the crash, the U.S. team had dominated figure skating. Now, the sport looked to a 15-year-old from Pasadena as its only hope.

By winning the national title, Peggy had qualified to compete in the 1964 Olympics, which were to be held in Innsbruck, Austria. Peggy realized that her chances for a medal were slim. "If I'm among the top 10, I'll be satisfied," she said. She got her wish; she came in sixth.

In June of 1965, Peggy moved to Colorado Springs, Colorado, so that she could work with Carlo Fassi, a famous Italian-born coach who had begun coaching at the Broadmoor Hotel's ice arena in 1961. Her dad got a job with the Colorado Springs newspaper so the rest of the family was able to make the move later that year. The Broadmoor had become, and still is, a training center for elite figure skaters.

After the 1961 plane crash that wiped out the U.S. team, Peggy became American skating's best hope.

The move to Colorado Springs helped Peggy in several ways: She could work with a top coach, she could train in the high altitude of Colorado Springs (more than 6,000 feet above sea level), and she could attend Cheyenne Mountain High School, which had a flexible class schedule. The 1966 world championships were to be held in Davos, Switzerland, which is also at a very high altitude.

JOHN G. ZIMMERMAN/SPORTS ILLUSTRATED

Because there is a lower level of oxygen in the air at high altitudes, it is harder for people to breathe—until they adjust to the altitude. But long-term high-altitude training helps athletes build endurance, and Peggy needed to build up her stamina.

Her schedule was tough. She practiced from 7 a.m. to 11 a.m., then went to school, and returned to the ice from 5 p.m. to 8 p.m. Peggy was a perfectionist who did not want to leave anything to chance. She spent hours practicing her school figures. "I suppose some of my skating skill is natural talent," she once said, "but mostly it's just hard work."

The new coach and the new altitude helped Peggy tremendously. Although she had had little formal ballet training, Peggy had a natural grace that Carlo Fassi polished by having her work with several skating choreographers.

In 1966, Peggy went to Davos to compete in the world championships. Defending champion Petra Burka, from Canada, was heavily favored to win. Peggy stunned Petra, however, by skating perfectly in the compulsory figures, which counted for 60 percent of the score. When the figures were over, Peggy led Petra by a whopping 49 points. "That's it," exclaimed a U.S. team official. "Unless Peggy falls flat on the ice, she's got it in the bag."

Peggy did not fall flat. Dressed in shocking pink, she leaped and spun to the strains of classical music with her usual grace—and her recently developed stamina. She included in her free skating program a combination that had become her trademark move: a spread-eagle glide into a double Axel jump, then back into a spread eagle. The move was difficult because Peggy took off for the jump with both feet on the ice, each foot pointing in the opposite direction. Most skaters take off on one foot with their body in a forward position when they perform an Axel.

The judges found Peggy's performance almost flawless. One judge awarded her a perfect 6.0, and Peggy became the new world champion!

Tenley Albright, the 1956 Olympic champion, watched Peggy's performance on television and was thrilled by what she saw. "Peggy has a lovely line to her body," said Tenley. "She is closer to the discipline that dancers have, and which skaters sometimes lack. Everyone comments on how easily she does things, and considering how hard a skater has to work to achieve them, that's just about the biggest compliment you can get. I just hope she goes on skating forever."

Peggy was, of course, excited by winning the world championship. But her spirit was soon dampened. Peggy and her mother, who always traveled with her, were preparing to return home from Europe when they received tragic news: Peggy's dad had died of a heart attack.

Peggy was saddened, and uncertain that she would be able to afford the cost of skating without her father's help. But the family encouraged Peggy to go on. In the end, Mr. Fleming's death only strengthened Peggy's resolve to win an Olympic gold medal. It was her dad's dream for her.

In 1967, Peggy won her fourth national championship and second world championship. She won that world title, in Vienna, Austria, despite falling as she leaped into a double Axel; she had built up such a commanding lead.

Peggy was favored to win the gold medal at the 1968 Olympics, which were to be held in Grenoble, France. That year she was a 19-year-old student at Colorado College in Colorado Springs. She could only take two classes a semester, however, because she was practicing seven hours every day for the Olympics.

When Ms. Fleming and Peggy arrived in Grenoble, there was a nasty flu going around the Olympic Village. Many of the competitors were coming down with it. Peggy, who always looked more frail than she actually was, moved out of the Village and into her mother's room in a hotel across from the Grenoble train station. "Peggy has a touch of sore throat, and she is nervous with all this pressure, you know," Ms. Fleming told a reporter at the Olympics.

Peggy seemed just fine, however, when she competed in the compulsory figures competition. More than fine—she ran up an overwhelming lead of 77 points, almost assuring her a gold medal.

Peggy had no reason to worry, but she couldn't help being nervous. This, after all, was *the Olympics*, and Peggy was expected to win the biggest prize. Even though she was only 19, she hoped to retire afterward because she was getting tired of the pressure of competitive skating. She wanted to go out on top.

JERRY COOKE/SPORTS ILLUSTRATED

At the 1968 Olympics, Peggy won the gold medal, Gabriele Seyfert the silver, and Hana Maskova the bronze.

F or her free skating program, Peggy chose to wear a chartreuse (lime-green) chiffon dress with rhinestones on its cuffs. The color seemed to fit the occasion: Chartreuse was the name of a greenish-yellow liqueur made by the monks of Grenoble.

But as she stepped out on the ice for her free skating program, Peggy caught the rhinestones on her sleeve against her beige tights. She became very nervous that her tights would run, and she had difficulty concentrating on her skating. At the last minute, she substituted a single Axel jump for a double, and she didn't complete the full two turns in her double Lutz.

By the time Peggy was halfway through her routine, Carlo Fassi had taken to hiding his eyes. The mistakes were barely noticeable to the average fan, yet when Peggy came off the ice, she burst into tears. She was a tough competitor, and she knew she had not skated her best.

Despite her errors, Peggy won the gold medal. She had a total score of 1,970.5, which was 88.2 points better than the silver medalist, Gabriele Seyfert of East Germany. (At that time, the country

of Germany was divided into the German Democratic Republic, called East Germany, and the Federal Republic of Germany, known as West Germany.) Peggy, who was already considered "America's sweetheart," endeared herself even more to the American public: She was the only American athlete to win a gold medal in Grenoble.

A few weeks after the Olympics, Peggy traveled to Geneva, Switzerland, to compete in the world championships. She easily won her third world title.

Afterward, she announced that she was retiring to concentrate on college. She said she wanted to become an elementary school teacher and hinted that she had a boyfriend. That boyfriend turned out to be Greg Jenkins, a Colorado College graduate who was attending medical school in Texas. Peggy married him two years later, in 1970. In 1971, their son was born.

Peggy never left the world of figure skating. Shortly after the Olympics, she signed a contract to appear in TV specials. And, over the years, she has toured with the Ice Follies and Holiday on Ice. She has also appeared as a guest with the Ice Capades. In 1981, she joined ABC-Sports as a figure skating commentator. She and Dick Button often cover skating events, including the Olympics, together.

No matter how accomplished a television commentator she becomes, however, Peggy Fleming will always be remembered for the grace and beauty that she brought to the sport—which no one else, before or since, has matched. "Peggy has no weaknesses," Gabriele Seyfert told a reporter after the 1968 Olympics. "On the ice, she is pure ballerina."

CHAPTER 8

John Curry

Against all odds, he showed the world that skating can be as much art as it is sport

When John Curry was a young boy growing up in England, he wanted to be a dancer. His parents weren't so keen on the idea; they thought he should try soccer or boxing. "My parents tried to steer me into something else," says John, "because dancing wasn't acceptable at the time for a boy." So, John took up the next best thing—figure skating—but he never lost his love for dance. Dance would influence his entire skating career, both as an amateur and as a pro.

John was born on September 9, 1949. He was the youngest of three sons, and his two older brothers were quite athletic. The Curry family lived in Birmingham, a working-class town 75 miles northwest of London.

When John was 6, he saw French skater Jacqueline Du Bief, the 1952 world champion, skate on television. He fell in love with figure skating, and begged his parents to sign him up for lessons. Six

months later, they did. His parents thought that skating was better than dancing, but they still didn't encourage John. They allowed him to skate once a week, for half an hour at a time—15 minutes of lessons and 15 minutes of practice.

John entered his first competition, called the "Hop, Skip and Jump" at his local rink that same year. Although he had spent so little time on the ice and performed a simple routine, with fewer "tricks" than the other children, he won because his skating showed unusual musical talent for someone so young. Even so, his parents refused to let him skate more often. "My parents viewed my skating with a sense of impending doom, believing there was no money in it," he once said. "They whisked me in and out of lessons so fast I never had the chance to roughhouse with other kids or pick up bad skating habits."

But John also didn't have enough time to master the complicated jumps and spins, which would cause problems for him later in his amateur career.

TONY TRIOLO/SPORTS ILLUSTRATED

John's skating was part sport, part dancing; he wanted to express the beauty of a body moving to music.

"I was not a wonder child technically," he says. When John was 11, he was allowed to spend a little more time at the rink, training under the rink's teacher, Ken Vickers.

As John's ice time increased, so did the number of his victories. He won many local competitions, but later said that he was more interested in bringing home prizes to set alongside his brothers' athletic awards than he was in beating other skaters.

When John was 16 in 1965, his father, a small business owner, accidentally shot himself and died. After his father's tragic death, John's mother was more willing to allow John to pursue his skating.

John left home, with almost no money, and moved to London to train with the world famous skating coach Arnold Gerschwiler. The two didn't always get along. John thought of himself as an artist, and he adjusted poorly to the strict and unbending personality of his coach. But John was still thrilled to be free to skate; in London, he also began to take ballet classes.

John now had to support himself. "I was on the ice from six a.m. until noon," John said. "After that I had to work, for a while at a supermarket, and later as a receptionist for National Cash Register, arranging demonstrations of computers. I must have been the sleepiest receptionist in the world."

For all of his sacrifices and hard work, though, John didn't have much to show for it. He was trying to skate in a new way, with more emphasis on the beauty of skating than on performing tricky jumps. Before John, male figure skaters were influenced by the success of Dick Button in the late 1940s and early '50s. They focused on athletics and on performing complicated jumps and spins.

John believed that figure skating was an art as well as a sport. In his free skating, he always tried to express the beauty of a body moving to music. So, while John glided across the ice with the grace and flourish of a ballet dancer, he didn't perform enough jumps to earn the respect of the judges. Or, when he did jump, he often fell. John worried that the judges would think that because his approach to skating was not terribly athletic, it was feminine.

"My style has been criticized because there is a school of thought that says skating is absolutely a sport," John once said. "That school says, 'Men should not use their arms; men should skate and basically just perform the athletic feats.' Everybody always said, 'John cannot do anything difficult,' but what I do is actually quite difficult."

Even so, John continued to earn low marks in competition. John's career began to change for the better in 1970, when he won the British championship. But the next year, at the world championships in Lyon, France, he skated so badly that he dreaded facing his coach and left the ice by a side entrance. In 1974, he won a bronze medal at the European championships but he again skated terribly at the world championships and finished seventh. It seemed that in emphasizing the artistic aspects of figure skating, John was neglecting the technical aspects he needed to impress the judges and score high marks. He was so frustrated that he was ready to give up skating for good.

But he didn't give up—thanks to Ed Mosler, a wealthy American skating fan whose family had started the Mosler Safe company. Ed saw John at the 1974 world championships, and offered to sponsor him, and bring him to the United States to train. Ed had helped many American skaters financially. He saw in John a potentially great skater who still needed a lot of work.

John accepted Ed's offer and his first stop in the U.S. was Lake Placid, New York, to work with Gus Lussi. Mr. Lussi had trained Dick Button many years earlier. John worked with Mr. Lussi for six months, long enough for the coach to straighten out John's jumping problems. Later that same year, 1974, John moved to Denver to work with Carlo Fassi, Peggy Fleming's former coach who was also coaching Dorothy Hamill.

Carlo Fassi tried not to change John's expressive style; he sought only to refine it. He added athletic elements to John's already artistic style. John also benefited from the encouragement his coach gave him. "Months before a major competition, Carlo starts telling everyone how good you are," John said. "Pretty soon you think so yourself."

It wasn't just his coach talking: John was actually becoming better. At the 1975 world championships in Colorado Springs, Colorado, he finished a much-improved third, behind Soviet skaters Sergei Volkov and Vladimir Kovalev.

John began to prepare in earnest for the 1976 Winter Olympics in Innsbruck, Austria. In the fall of 1975, he took a course in positive thinking, which helped him realize that he was a very good skater, capable of winning performances. Self-confidence always had been a problem for

At the 1976 Olympics, John won the gold medal, Vladimir Kovalev the silver, and Toller Cranston the bronze.

John because he hadn't received much support for his style of skating. But that was changing.

The 1976 European championships in Geneva, Switzerland, gave skating fans a glimpse of what was to come from John at the Olympics. But it also displayed the ugly politics that often lurk behind the judging in figure skating. Before the championships even had begun, Carlo Fassi had advised John to with-

draw. Five of the European's nine judges that year were from Eastern bloc countries. Those were countries in Eastern Europe that had Communist governments, which were under the influence of the Soviet Union and which strictly controlled the activities of their citizens. Mr. Fassi didn't think John would be judged fairly and he was right. The Soviet and Eastern European judges preferred the athletic style of skating, and they

TONY TRIOLO/SPORTS ILLUSTRATED

wanted Vladimir Kovalev of the U.S.S.R. to win.

Even though John skated beautifully, four of the "Communist" judges placed the Russian skater first. But one, from Czechoslovakia, placed John first. That vote, along with those of the four "Western" judges, gave John the votes he needed to win the European championship.

At the 1976 Olympics in Innsbruck, however, the judges were from all over the world, and John had a chance to be scored more fairly. After the compulsory competition, John was in the lead, much to the dismay of the Soviet officials, who hoped that Vladimir Kovalev, would win. A rumor began to spread that John planned to add an extra move to his short program. The short program, which counted for 20 percent of the total score, was a two-minute program in which the skater performed seven required freestyle moves, such as jumps or spins. (It had been added after the 1972 Olympics, with the compulsories reduced to first 40 percent and then 30 percent of the final score.) John wanted to make his short program extraordinary, so he planned to add a difficult double Axel from a spread-eagle position.

"The Soviets were concerned that I might do well at Innsbruck," John recalled, "so they were going around criticizing my program and telling judges, 'You can really nail Curry on this move.' It was not a pleasant situation, I must admit, so Carlo finally said, 'we'll just take the move out of the program, but we won't tell anyone that we're taking it out.'"

Carlo's strategy worked, and John kept the lead as he entered the free skating competition. For the free skating, John chose music written for the ballet *Don Quixote*. He wore a simple black outfit that showed how gracefully he moved his body. He skated with a slowness and perfect control that is rarely seen, and he included enough jumps to please the judges.

Like Peggy Fleming, John wove his jumps into his skating so beautifully that he made the performance look effortless. Dick Button, then working as the figure skating television commentator, called John's program "one of skating's great performances."

After many difficult years, John finally won the gold medal. Vladimir Kovalev won the silver, and Toller Cranston, a Canadian, the bronze. A few weeks later, John went to Göteborg, Sweden, and won the world championship. He had made a complete sweep of the figure skating titles—the European, the Olympics and the world.

For John, though, an Olympic gold medal was just a means to an end. His real dream had always been to form his own ice skating company, in which the sport could be pushed to its artistic limits. Now he was able to create that company, and he invited 11 other skaters to join him. He also asked famous dance choreographers to help create routines. Twyla Tharp, a New York modern dance choreographer, Peter Martins, then the principal dancer with the New York City Ballet, and Kenneth MacMillan, of Great Britain's Royal Ballet, each created a piece for him. In 1978, John brought his entire show, called *Ice Dancing*, to the United States.

The show forced skating audiences to reconsider figure skating. In *Ice Dancing*, skaters performed dance movements rather than only the jumps and spins of competitive figure skating. And *Ice Dancing* was more understated than other ice shows.

"Traditional ice shows camouflage the quality of skating," John told *People* magazine in 1979. "Just when the artistic part of one's career should begin, a skater ruins it by joining revues like Ice Capades or [Ice] Follies. Skating is not the primary concern of those shows—they are wrapped up in the razzmatazz and glitter." Earlier, he had said, "I'm trying to present skating in a way it's never been presented before." John succeeded in doing that. He presented his unique ice shows well into the 1980s.

John always worked to push the limits of skating as an art form. "Skating isn't simply tricks. But it's not ballet either," he said in an interview in 1978. "I'm an ice skater, and the innate qualities of skating—the glide, the lack of friction—can't be duplicated in any other form."

John loved skating, and that love showed every time he performed. But his love for dance was just as strong. Because he admired dance so much, he raised men's figure skating to another level.

CHAPTER 9

Dorothy Hamill

When the pressure was greatest, she turned stage fright into stardom

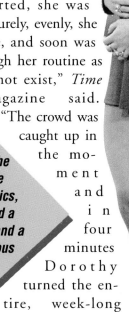

Even though she was an immensely talented skater, Dorothy Hamill experienced terrible stage fright before every competition. When she was very young, she would get sick to her stomach before it was her turn to skate.

Like all true champions, however, Dorothy rarely buckled when the pressure was on. When she began to skate, her nerves faded away. Nowhere was this more apparent than at the 1974 world championships in Munich, West Germany, when she was 17 years old.

Dorothy was warming up at the end of the rink, waiting to be introduced for her free skating program. But she couldn't start because the crowd was booing so loudly that she wouldn't have been able to hear her music. Dorothy thought that the crowd was yelling at *her*, and she fled the ice to cry in her father's arms. In truth, the crowd was booing the judges; the audience thought that the skater who had performed before Dorothy had been given scores that were much too low.

After realizing that the jeers had not been aimed at her, Dorothy stopped her crying, collected herself, and skated back onto the ice. And once the music started, she was transformed. "Surely, evenly, she started to skate, and soon was sweeping through her routine as if gravity did not exist," *Time* magazine said.

"The crowd was caught up in the moment and in four minutes Dorothy turned the entire, week-long

By the end of the 1976 Olympics, Dorothy had a gold medal and a world-famous haircut.

TONY TRIOLO/SPORTS ILLUSTRATED

championship into her show."

Dorothy did not win the world championship that year—the honor went to Christine Errath of East Germany—but she had given the championships' single most exciting performance. She finished second.

That was typical of the way it was with Dorothy. When she was able to relax on the ice, she was a wonderful figure skater. Just 5'3" and 110 pounds, Dorothy was nonetheless a powerful skater. She could perform impressive jumps without much noticeable exertion, which is quite unusual among women skaters, and then land lightly on her blades. She was well-known for her spins, which were fast yet delicate. She even introduced a spin of her own, now known as the Hamill camel, in which she went from a flying camel spin into a back sit spin. Most of all, Dorothy had a feel for the music to which she skated. Her body moved in perfect rhythm to the music.

When Dorothy skated well, even she was inspired. "You're skating and doing the most difficult things," she once said, "and the audience is with you. They're clapping, cheering. You're floating. It's like nothing else I've ever felt."

When Dorothy first began to skate, all she wanted to do was learn how to skate backwards. It was 1965, and Dorothy was 8 years old. She had just received a pair of skates for Christmas from her parents, Chalmers and Carol Hamill. Dorothy and her friends went to skate on a pond near their home in Riverside, Connecticut, a town not far from New York City. "A bunch of us were at the pond, and the others could skate backwards, but I couldn't," said Dorothy. "I wanted to learn, so my mother signed me up for group lessons."

Dorothy progressed quickly, and she soon switched to private lessons. When she was 10, she began to enter competitions and when she was 12, she won the 1969 novice women's championship. When she was 14, Dorothy finished seventh overall at the 1971 world championships.

Figure skating is a very expensive sport, and Dorothy's training was no exception. Her father made a good salary as an engineer, but in the years preceding the 1976 Olympics, Dorothy's training, travel, and equipment cost the family $10,000 to $15,000 a year. That might have been okay if Dorothy were the only child in the Hamill family, but she isn't. She has a brother, Sandy, who is five years older, and a sister, Marcia, who is two years older. "Every time she got on the ice," Carol Hamill once told *People* magazine, "she did so well that we just couldn't say, 'Sorry, honey, we can't afford it, you'll have to quit.'"

The cost to the Hamill family could not be measured only in dollars. They were often separated because of Dorothy's career, both for competitions and for training. When Dorothy was 14, she and her mother decided to move to Denver, Colorado, so that Dorothy could work with Carlo Fassi, the famous coach who had trained Peggy Fleming. Dorothy quit her formal schooling at that point, and continued her high school studies with private tutors. Chalmers Hamill stayed in Connecticut. "He has to make the money to help me skate," Dorothy said.

Dorothy spent long days at the ice rink skating with Carlo Fassi. Under her coach's watchful eye, she began skating at 7 a.m. every day, and skated for seven hours, breaking only for lunch. She skated six days a week, for 11 months a year. On her one day off a week, she studied ballet. Her only real breaks came when she took two weeks off in the spring and two weeks off in the fall. She kept up with this grueling schedule for four years.

Dorothy knew that she was sacrificing a "normal" high school life, but she didn't mind. "I don't even know what it's like to be normal," Dorothy joked to a reporter once, "but I've never really found anything I liked to do as much as skating."

On the ice, Dorothy's sacrifices paid off. In 1973, she was runner-up at the national championships to

Dorothy's back-stage jitters vanished soon after she took the ice. She was transformed by music.

TONY TRIOLO/SPORTS ILLUSTRATED

Janet Lynn, the five-time U.S. champion. It was clear that Dorothy was now viewed by the judges as Janet's successor.

In 1974, after Janet retired, Dorothy became the new national champion at the U.S. championships in Providence, Rhode Island. The American judges wanted her to be the new U.S. champion so badly that they overlooked an error in one of her compulsory figures, and placed her first. Then they gave her very high scores—5.8's and 5.9's—for a uninspired free skating program. They did

Although small in size, Dorothy was a powerful skater. She was known for her spins, which were very fast yet delicate.

that because they wanted her to receive high scores at the world championships later that year, and low scores from American judges could very possibly mean low scores from international judges. (Previous scores, particularly those of national championships, carry a lot of weight among international judges.) That year's world championship was the one in which Dorothy skated brilliantly after bursting into tears, and finished in second place.

Dorothy proved to be a worthy successor to Janet Lynn. She won the national championship in 1975 and again in 1976. The Olympic figure skating team was chosen after the '76 national championships in Colorado Springs, Colorado, so it was a particularly important competition. Everyone expected Dorothy to win, but her coach was watching closely to see how well she would *perform*. The short program was a breeze. *Sports Illustrated* wrote that her "two

minutes of ice time [were] fiery, clean and admirable." But in her long program, Dorothy made some mistakes and lacked flair. She leaned badly on a double Axel early in her program, and never quite recovered. She left several jumps out of the program, which made Carlo Fassi crazy.

The judges, who wanted her to be judged well at the Olympics, again gave Dorothy high scores of 5.8's and 5.9's. Dorothy knew better, though. "Much too high," she muttered as the scores were posted. "I'll show a lot more at the Olympics," she told reporters.

Dorothy had let the tension get to her and, at the nationals, she had suffered from nerves. "It's like an execution," Dorothy told *Time* magazine, "your own. I stand there in the dressing room thinking, 'Am I going to fall? Why am I doing this?'"

Dorothy brought plenty of things with her to each competition to make her feel comfortable. She had two good-luck pins—a four-leaf clover and a jeweled fly—that she attached to her skating outfits. She had a collection of stuffed animals—a koala, duck, lamb, monkey, and turtle—and a Raggedy Ann doll that she kept at rinkside. And most important of all, she had her father, who always stood by her before she went out on the ice in competitions to give her a hug or help her out by making last minute adjustments to her skates.

Most skating spectators never realized how much Dorothy was plagued by jitters. They saw her as a beautiful skater with a brilliant smile and a great haircut. Dorothy's haircut, a wedge cut, became so popular that people began to call it "the

TONY TRIOLO/SPORTS ILLUSTRATED

Hamill cut." Skating fans also saw Dorothy as the next Peggy Fleming. There was something to the comparisons; both skaters were fluid, musical, and graceful, and both were coached by Carlo Fassi. "Dorothy is stronger, more athletic," said Mr. Fassi. "Peggy was more artistic. But both are tremendous fighters and strong performers."

America pinned its gold medal hopes on Dorothy for the 1976 Olympics in Innsbruck, Austria. Dorothy expected her biggest competition to come from Dianne de Leeuw, a California skater who held both American and Dutch citizenships but skated for the Dutch team. Dorothy knew how good Dianne was because Dorothy had been runner-up to her at the 1975 world championships.

Dorothy knew that she would have to gain an early lead in the compulsory figures, her weakest event, to have a chance at the gold. She did just that; she was in second place after the compulsories, ahead of Dianne. Her short program was flawless and impassioned, and her scores were good enough to bump her into first place.

For the long program, Dorothy chose, with her parents' help, to skate to the musical scores that had come from several different Errol Flynn movies. Errol Flynn was a popular actor who starred in a number of adventure movies in the 1940s. Dorothy skated in a simple, low cut red dress; red was her favorite color.

She began the routine with one of her best moves, a delayed Axel, in which she leapt into the air and appeared to hang there for a split second before beginning the Axel's one and a half turns. She finished with another one of her best moves, the Hamill camel.

"Dorothy gave the kind of performance that marks her distinctive style: she rushed brightly through the air in long, effortless leaps and then spun endlessly, it seemed, on a still point," according to the story of the event that ran in *Time* magazine. When the music stopped, the enthusiastic audience showered her with flowers, which she picked up as she skated off the ice.

Dorothy was nearsighted, and she had to squint to see her scores. But she liked what she saw: a solid line of 5.9's for artistic impression. "I didn't really bomb out on anything," Dorothy said in her dressing room later. "That's a first for me!"

Dianne, who performed after Dorothy, skated well but couldn't overcome Dorothy's lead. Dorothy received first place votes from all nine judges, and won the gold medal. During the awards ceremony, Dorothy fingered the gold medal as though she weren't sure it was real. She took the medal with her to dinner that evening, and she slept with it under her pillow. She had to convince herself that this long-held dream had come true.

Her next stop after the Olympics was Göteborg, Sweden, where Dorothy won her first world championship. After that, she signed a contract to skate in the Ice Capades for an estimated $2 million dollars. The ice show work involved long hours and a lot of travel, but Dorothy wanted to earn enough money to begin to pay back her parents for the financial sacrifices they had made.

Dorothy stayed in the news—but more for what she did off the ice than on it. Shortly after the Olympics, she began to date Dean Paul Martin, the handsome son of actor Dean Martin. Young Dean had been a struggling professional tennis player, auto racer, and sometime actor. In 1981, he and Dorothy were married; their wedding was attended by celebrities such as singer Frank Sinatra and tennis player Jimmy Connors. But the marriage didn't last. They were divorced only 21 months later. In 1987, Dorothy married Kenneth Forsythe, a doctor in Los Angeles whose specialty, appropriately enough, was sports medicine. They had a daughter the following year.

Dorothy still skates as a guest star in ice shows and on television specials. She no longer suffers from the terrible nerves that plagued her as an amateur. Now she concentrates more on the joy of skating, without the pressure. "I love the feeling of freedom—the jumping, the spinning. You feel like a bird flying through the air," she has said. "It's such a great feeling to be out there."

CHAPTER 10

Robin Cousins

The grace of a dancer and the power of an athlete combined to produce a champion

Robin Cousins was the natural successor to John Curry, the 1976 Olympic champion. Like John, Robin was English, and he had wanted to be a dancer as a boy. Robin, however, combined great athleticism with his love of dance. But before he became a champion, he had to travel a hard road, too.

Robin put on his first skates when he was almost 8 years old, while he and his family were on a summer vacation at the seashore. One hot day, Robin's dad and his two brothers went to the beach, and Robin and his mom decided to look at the shops in town. They passed an ice rink, and because it was so hot, they decided to go in and cool off.

Mrs. Cousins rented skates for Robin, and was helping him get ready when she asked a nearby stranger if he could explain the basics of skating to Robin. She discovered that the stranger was a skating instructor who would be happy to teach Robin—if Mrs. Cousins paid for it. Mrs. Cousins barely had enough money for the lesson, but she was too embarrassed to back out. In his first lesson,

Robin skated so well that the instructor could not believe that this was his first time on ice.

Robin wasn't surprised. He had been taking ballet lessons since he was 6, and he was a graceful boy. While his older brothers played soccer, cricket, and rugby, Robin preferred the artistic qualities of ballet and, later, skating. "I like movement," Robin said. "I began by simply leaping up in the air and spinning and turning, not wondering how or where I was going to land. I guess my style grew from that point." He began taking private skating lessons at a rink in his hometown of Bristol when he was 10.

Before Robin was 12, he received a scholarship offer from the Royal Ballet School, in London, which was 125 miles away from home. Robin wasn't ready to move so far away from his family, so he turned down the offer and began focus-

Robin was lackluster at practice, but when he skated before an audience he was an inspired performer.

HEINZ KLUETMEIER/SPORTS ILLUSTRATED

ing all his energies on skating.

In 1970, when he was 13, Robin won the British primary championship. In 1972, he won the British junior championship. That same year, Robin finished third in the British senior competition. He was an unpolished skater, but his jumps were daring and high. People could see that he had potential.

GEORGE TIEDEMANN/SPORTS ILLUSTRATED

A pioneer among skaters, Robin selected his program, chose his music, and even designed his outfit.

Robin had gone as far as he could under his coach in Bristol. In order to improve as a skater, he knew he would have to leave his family. Just before his 17th birthday, Robin moved to London to study under Gladys Hogg, a famous skating coach. The move was not easy. "It was the nightmare of my life," Robin recalled several years later. He would walk to the rink at 5 a.m., skate for a couple of hours, and then work stocking shelves in a grocery store in order to pay for his skating lessons and $14-a-week rent. "I was living in what amounted to a converted closet," he said.

Robin's life was difficult, but once he was on the ice, he thought it was worth it. He loved skating, and he wanted to become a champion. But first he had to improve his compulsory figures and acquire the polish that comes only with experience. With every year, he came closer to his goal. In 1975, Robin was runner-up to John Curry in the British championships. The second-place finish didn't tell the whole story, though. John had fallen during his free skating program, and Robin won that portion of the competition, achieving one of his goals. He had always wanted to beat John in the free skating competition because John was Britain's best skater

and was known internationally for his elegant free skating programs.

At the 1976 Olympics in Innsbruck, Austria, however, Robin was overlooked by the international judges. This frequently happens to a newcomer. No matter how talented he may be, it is hard to be taken seriously by the judges the first time around. Robin skated well, but John was the star of those Olympics—and the gold medal winner. One German journalist wrote jokingly that Robin skated to the music of *Three Blind Mice* (he hadn't) in front of nine blind judges. Robin finished in 10th place.

In the fall of 1976, after John had turned professional, Robin became the new British champion. He looked forward to competing with greater respect from the international judges now that he was out of John's shadow. But in December, Robin tore cartilage, the tissue that connects bone to bone, in his knee, and had to have surgery. Robin couldn't stand the thought of losing an entire season to an injury, so he continued to practice.

Even though the knee still gave him pain, Robin decided to enter the world championships in Tokyo, Japan, in the spring of 1977. Gladys Hogg, Robin's coach, was afraid to fly and didn't accompany him. Carlo Fassi, the Colorado-based coach who had trained Peggy Fleming and John Curry, helped Robin while he was in Japan. Despite performing in agonizing pain, Robin was in sixth place before the free skating competition began. Halfway through his routine, however, his knee gave out completely, and he had to leave the ice. He was humiliated.

One good thing came of that trip. Robin was so impressed by Carlo Fassi's coaching that he decided to move to Denver, Colorado, later that year to train with him, just as John Curry had done. He thought Mr. Fassi would be able to improve his skating even more.

That year, Robin also set goals for himself which would end, he hoped, with the 1980 Olympic gold medal. He wanted to win a bronze medal at the '78 world championships, a silver at the '79 worlds, and then the gold medal.

He competed in the 1978 world championships in Ottawa, Canada, and finished third. The three top skaters—Charlie Tickner, an American; Jan Hoffmann, an East German; and Robin—were so close to one another in points, though, that it was almost a three-way tie.

In the spring of 1979, Robin again finished where he had hoped—with a silver medal in the world championships. This time it was Robin's turn as the senior skater to get special treatment from the judges. "The judges virtually bent over backwards for Robin," said John Curry. "I think they wanted him to win. But he just didn't perform well in the compulsories." Vladimir Kovalev, a perfectionist in compulsories, won the world title.

The compulsory figures had always given Robin trouble. Still, he never seemed all that interested in working at them. He loved the free skating—the high jumps, the fast spins, the dance moves—and the crowds that went with it. "Without the crowd," he once said, "there is no inspiration."

Robin was considered the finest free skater in the world at the time—

when he wanted to be. He loved to skate before an audience, but wasn't always willing to work hard in practice. This infuriated Carlo Fassi.

At the British championships in 1979, Robin attempted a triple jump during his long program, and fell. "After that, I couldn't get back into it," he said. "Every time I went toward a triple, I thought about it, and I chickened out." At the European championships in Göteborg, Sweden, in January of 1980, Robin once again turned his planned triple jump into a double during his short program. Carlo Fassi shouted from the rinkside, "You are chicken!"

That was all 22-year-old Robin needed to hear. When he came back for the free skating, he landed not one but three triple jumps—and won the European championships for the first time ever. Still, Mr. Fassi wasn't impressed. "You did just enough to win the European," he told Robin. "But that kind of performance won't win at Lake Placid."

Lake Placid, New York, was where the 1980 Olympics were to be held. Robin did not plan to fail when he got there. He had spent hours choosing music, choreographing much of his routines, and simply practicing.

Although most skaters help create their skating routines,

Robin's road led him through poverty in London, to the U.S. for coaching, to Lake Placid for the gold medal.

Robin had more input than usual. And his taste in skating music was not traditional. In fact, Robin deserves credit for pushing skating music into the modern era. "I decide what I want to do," he said, "and Carlo de-

ENRICO FERORELLI/SPORTS ILLUSTRATED

cides how it best fits into the program." For his Olympic programs, he combined disco music with classical music. He even designed his own free skating costume, a black pants outfit with sequins.

There were four favorites for the 1980 competition: Robin; Vladimir Kovalev, the 1979 world champ; Charlie Tickner, the 1978 world champ; and Jan Hoffmann, the 1974 world champ from East Germany, who had almost won in 1978.

Kovalev dropped out after placing fifth in the compulsory figures. Jan Hoffmann was in first place, Charlie Tickner was second, and Robin was fourth. "I don't think anyone has won the Olympics who hasn't placed in the top three in figures," declared Charlie's coach, Norma Sahlin, in an obvious dig at Robin. She was right about the past, but there is a first time for everything.

After the compulsories, Robin skated brilliantly in the short program, and moved into second place, behind Jan. Charlie, meanwhile, skated poorly and fell into fifth place. Robin became the man to beat in the free skating. Jan was not considered to be as elegant, or as entertaining, a free skater.

Four and half million television viewers in Great Britain stayed awake until 4 a.m.—it is six hours later there—to watch Robin's long program. They weren't disappointed. Robin started out with a flawless camel spin, and moved through a routine that was punctuated with disco music and disco moves. He finished his routine with a fast open Axel (meaning that his legs were apart) into a sit spin—a dramatic conclusion to an otherwise, for Robin, conservative program. But the nine judges were impressed, and eight awarded Robin 5.9's for artistic impression.

Jan skated after Robin. He also skated flawlessly, but lacked Robin's creative flair. Jan received almost the same scores as Robin—5.8's and 5.9's—for technical merit, but his scores for artistic impression were considerably lower. Jan's point total was higher than Robin's for the three event competition, but in the complicated scoring of figure skating, which relies not on point totals but on what place in the standings the most judges put you, Robin still won. Robin was placed first by five judges, while Jan received first place votes from only three judges. Robin had won the gold medal!

Robin's only fall of the Olympics came when he stumbled while walking the one and a half steps up to the victory platform. Robin could barely contain his joy at winning, and as the British flag rose over the victory stand, he caught his parents' eyes in the stands. "We were looking directly at each other," he said. "I was able to know how they were feeling, and they could see how I was feeling, but it is difficult to describe that to anyone else." One thing is sure: Robin's parents, Fred and Jo Cousins, were proud.

Jan took his revenge by beating Robin at the world championships in West Germany a few weeks later. Shortly after that, Robin became a professional skater. He still skates as a featured guest in ice shows and television specials, but now he's also busy as the artistic director of the Ice Castle International Training Center, in Southern California. The center has two rinks, a dance studio, and dormitories for young skaters, so that they can have an easier time of their training than Robin did.

Robin doesn't regret his hardships, though. "They made me far more determined," he says. "I would be crying and saying, 'I can't do this!' Then, I'd go back on the ice and say, 'This is great!'" When it was all over, when the Olympic competition had ended, even the worst hardships didn't seem so bad. Robin had turned tough times into gold.

CHAPTER 11

Scott Hamilton

A sickly child who couldn't play sports, he took up skating and became the best

When young Scott Hamilton took his first wobbly steps onto the ice, in 1965, no one could have predicted that he would become the 1984 Olympic figure skating champion. The people who watched him weren't even sure Scott would be able to skate the length of the rink.

Scott was a tiny 9-year-old who had been weakened by years of illness. He couldn't eat normally, so he had a feeding tube that went to his stomach; the other end of it came out through his nose. When he wasn't using the tube, he draped it across his cheek and taped it behind his ear.

Scott was born on August 28, 1958, and adopted six weeks later by Ernie and Dorothy Hamilton of Bowling Green, Ohio, both professors at Bowling Green University. The Hamiltons had one child of their own, Susan, who was five years older than Scott. Four years after they adopted

Scott, they adopted another son, Steve.

When the Hamiltons picked up Scott from the adoption agency, he was a cute, healthy baby. When Scott was two, however, he suddenly stopped growing. The Hamiltons took Scott to many doctors. One said Scott was allergic to certain foods, so the family put him on a special diet. "That meant that he literally starved for two or three years," says Scott's dad. Some of the specialists thought Scott might have cystic fibrosis, an inherited disease that can be fatal. One doctor said that Scott had only six months to live. Out of desperation, the Hamiltons took Scott to Boston's famous Children's Hospital,

Because he wanted skating to be respected as a sport, Scott skated in a simple stretch suit, with no beads or spangles.

MANNY MILAN/SPORTS ILLUSTRATED

Blairsville High School Library

which was known for its advanced cystic fibrosis research. Doctors there said he didn't have cystic fibrosis but a related condition called Shwachman's syndrome. In Scott's case, he wasn't able to digest food. So, in order for him to grow, he would have to use a feeding tube.

Scott began to gain strength. Because he had been in and out of hospitals for most of his young life, he had never been able to play sports, like most kids. But then, when Scott was 9, Susan took him along to an ice skating rink to watch while she skated. "You know," he told his family, "I think I'd like to try skating."

He started out a little shaky. "Whenever I let go of the barrier," Scott told *The New York Times* in 1983, "I fell down. I cried a lot when I fell, but I got used to it. After a few sessions, the club pros said I might be good, and they asked my parents to bring me in for lessons." The Hamiltons wanted to encourage Scott as much as they could, so they enrolled him in skating lessons.

The cold air and exercise appeared to work miracles. During his checkup the next year, the doctor said to Mrs. Hamilton, "What have you done to this boy? He's healthy!" Scott had actually begun to grow. But Scott would never make up all the growing he had missed. By the time he reached adulthood, he was still small—5'3½".

Scott was teased a lot as a child because he was so much smaller than his classmates. He couldn't keep up with the other children in a lot of their activities. But in skating he could be better than all of them.

As Scott improved as a skater, he realized that he would need a better coach than those available in Bowling Green. So, when he was 13, Scott moved to Illinois to work with Pierre Brunet, who had trained 1960 Olympic champion Carol Heiss and 1962 world champion Donald Jackson. It was not an easy move; Scott was very close to his parents, and he missed them. But his new coach helped his skating career tremendously. In 1976, he won the United States juniors championship.

Scott loved the sport of figure skating and wanted to continue, but the cost was becoming too much for his parents. "My folks had spent all the money they could possibly afford," Scott said. "So I decided to quit skating and start college at Bowling Green." Just then, however, a wealthy couple, who were great fans of figure skating, offered to take care of Scott's training and expenses. (They preferred to remain anonymous.)

That fall, Scott moved to Denver to work with Carlo Fassi, who had coached Peggy Fleming and Dorothy Hamill. In 1977, tragedy struck Scott's life when his mother died of cancer. Scott was crushed. His mother had always stood by him, during his sickness and during his rise as a skater. "I felt so guilty," Scott said. "She was so giving and terrific, and I didn't do my best as a skater."

After her death, Scott dedicated himself to becoming a world-class skater. At the 1977 national championships, the last time his mother saw him compete, Scott finished ninth. In 1978, he finished third. When he failed to qualify for the world championships in 1979, he decided that Mr. Fassi had too many other students to give him all the attention he needed. Carlo Fassi was now coaching Robin Cousins as well as Scott, so Scott decided to leave him for another coach, Don Laws. He never looked for another coach again. Don Laws pushed Scott hard to achieve perfection, and that was exactly what Scott wanted. No matter how hard his coach pushed him, Scott pushed himself even harder.

In 1980, Scott finished third in the national championships, which qualified him to compete in both the Olympics and the world championships. The Olympics were being held in Lake Placid, New York. Although Scott was not expected to win any medals, the team picked him to carry the American flag at the opening ceremonies. In the Olympic figure skating competition, Robin Cousins

Scott thought men's skating had become too much like ballet. His style was athletic and aggressive.

BILL EPPRIDGE/SPORTS ILLUSTRATED

won the gold medal, and Scott finished fifth. It was to be the last time Scott lost during his competitive career.

In 1981, Scott's father came out to San Diego, California, to watch him compete in the national championships. Two days before the men's finals however, Mr. Hamilton suffered a mild stroke, but he didn't tell Scott. After wishing Scott good luck on the day of the finals, he checked into the hospital. Scott won the title and then learned of his father's stroke. "I asked myself, When is it going to end?" Scott said. "Couldn't I have something good, and be happy, without something bad?"

Because of his father's illness, Scott almost skipped the world championships, which were to be held four weeks later in Hartford, Connecticut. At the last minute, though, Scott decided to go—and he won! It was a very emotional victory.

Scott was proud to be winning, but he also wanted to do more: He wanted to change the image of men's figure skating. Scott thought that the sport had become too much like ballet; his own style was much more athletic.

Although Scott was small, he was surprisingly strong. "It ain't much," he often joked about his small body, "but everything I've got here is skating muscle." Scott used all of those muscles to skate at great speeds, and perform one difficult jump after another in his free skating programs. He performed all of his jumps and spins with textbook-perfect technique. "On the ice," said Don Laws, "Scott is aggressive—but never abandoned. He's always in control, never angled wrong. Everything about him—his stance, his actions, his body—says 'skater.'"

Because Scott wanted figure skating to be respected as a *sport*, he stopped wearing fancy skating costumes with beads and spangles all over them. "Some of the skaters look like a Las Vegas lounge act," Scott once complained. He preferred to wear a plain stretch suit, similar to the one worn by U.S. speed skaters.

The figure skating judges didn't care what Scott wore; they just continued to be impressed by how he skated. He won the national and world championships in 1982. Then, in 1983, he won them again, becoming the first American man to win three consecutive world championships since David Jenkins accomplished that feat between 1957 and 1959.

No American man had won an Olympic figure skating gold medal since David Jenkins had won one in Squaw Valley, California, in 1960. Now, America turned its eyes to Scott as its best hope for another gold.

Scott warmed up for the Olympics at the 1984 national championships in Salt Lake City, Utah, where his performance drew a perfect score of 6.0 from four of the nine judges. Scott was considered such a shoo-in for the gold medal that another American skater, Mark Cockerell, told a reporter that Scott could only lose "if he threw himself on his back and rolled around."

But Scott wanted more than the gold medal. He wanted to give the performance of his life. He had already completely dominated men's figure skating; now he hoped to take his skating one level higher. He started spending six hours a day on the ice, practicing. "I want to give the best performance I can, so that there will be no regrets," he said. "I want to make sure I do everything I can and skate as well as I can."

Shortly after he arrived in Sarajevo, Yugoslavia, for the 1984 Winter Olympics, Scott came down with a cold and an ear infection. The cold wasn't a problem, but the ear infection affected Scott's sense of balance. He began to take antibiotics and hoped that he would recover quickly.

Scott won the Olympic compulsory competition, which counted for 30 percent of the total score. That surprised him; he usually came in second or third in compulsories, and made up for it in his free skating. As it turned out, he would need the big lead from the compulsories to win the gold.

Brian Orser, the Canadian champion, won the short program, which counted for 20 percent of the total score. That put Brian in fifth place. If he skated brilliantly in the free skating, he could be a threat to

Scott for the gold medal.

Sure enough, Brian skated a knockout free skating program that included a triple Axel, which Scott didn't perform in competition. Brian performed three triple jumps in his routine—and earned eight 5.9's and one 5.8 from the nine judges.

Scott skated next. His free skating program started with American jazz music, and he opened with a perfect camel spin. Scott had planned to do five triple jumps, but, his balance was off from the ear infection and he was only able to complete three of them. And the three he completed had wobbly landings.

The next part of Scott's routine was skated to Oriental music, an eerie selection played mostly on electronic synthesizers. Scott skated slowly for the next couple of minutes, breaking into a waltz at one point. It was a move usually associated more with ice dancing, which features skating to different tempos, than men's figure skating, but Scott performed it with a comic touch, which the audience loved.

Scott's body was small, but strong, "Everything I've got here is skating muscle," he once said.

HEINZ KLUETMEIER/SPORTS ILLUSTRATED

The last minute of the program was supposed to be classic Scott Hamilton—meaning he would put on a display of his characteristic fast and aggressive skating. Scott planned to perform a double Axel, double Lutz, split jump, and double Salchow, finishing with a spin so fast that he would become a blur. He pulled it off, but not with his usual precision. After Scott had finished skating, he said, "I felt like I had a 10-pound weight around each ankle." To Don Laws, his coach and good friend, Scott could only say, "I'm sorry."

Scott didn't have to apologize. He finished second in the free skating program to Brian Orser, with one 5.9, three 5.8's, two 5.7's, and three 5.6's. And because he had built up such a lead in the compulsories, he won the gold medal.

Scott, who later won his fourth world championship and then became a professional skater, took a moment to reflect after his Olympic win. "The whole last four years have been for this night," he told reporters. "I've worked so hard, trained so hard, waited so long. I wanted it to be special. I wanted it to be my greatest program. It wasn't my best, but I did it."

Scott underestimated his accomplishment. He seemed to have forgotten how far he had traveled just to get to the Olympics. Only 18 years earlier, Scott's parents weren't sure he would live, let alone play sports. Now he was the best skater in the world.

CHAPTER 12

Brian Boitano

His biggest hurdle wasn't jumping; it was learning to put his soul on ice

RICHARD MACKSON/SPORTS ILLUSTRATED

Brian Boitano was only 8 years old when he took his first group ice skating lesson from Linda Leaver. But, even then, Ms. Leaver could see that Brian had natural ability. "I came home and told my husband I was teaching someone who could be world champion some day," she said. She was right: Brian would grow up to become a two-time world champion *and* the 1988 Olympic gold medal winner.

The youngest of four Boitano children, Brian's first try at skating was on *roller* skates when he was 5 years old. He performed on the sidewalks in front of his home in Sunnyvale, California, a town in the San Francisco Bay area. "I liked speed, things that go fast," Brian recalled. "I was out on my skates five or six hours a day, and my parents started worrying that I might crack my skull when I began jumping into the air, trying to do Axels."

Brian's parents thought that ice skating might be safer, so they took him to the Sunnyvale Ice Palace and signed him up for lessons. "Like most boys, Brian was never very interested in the artistic side,

how you point your toe and all that," Ms. Leaver told *Sports Illustrated* in 1988. "He was interested in going fast and jumping high and doing more turns than everybody else."

Brian entered, and won, his first competition, a local pixie boys division event, the first year he started ice skating. By the time he was 12, Brian had already won 17 medals from local and regional competitions. He began to devote more and more time to training. When Brian finished his high school studies, he decided to skip college and skate full-time. Brian's dad was a successful banker who could afford to support his son's full-time skating. The U.S. Figure Skating Association also agreed to sponsor Brian, covering part of his travel expenses.

In 1982, when Brian was 18, he became the first man ever to land a triple Axel—three and half full turns in the air—at the U.S. nationals. Brian was a

> **I**n the '88 Olympics, Brian dressed as a soldier and skated to music from the movie "Napoleon."

very consistent skater who prided himself on being able to accomplish difficult technical moves. He was so interested in pushing the athletic limits of figure skating, though, that he often ignored the artistic side of the sport. "I was like a little technical robot," he once said. "I never missed. And the reason I never missed was that I never put any energy into my presentation."

The artistic part of skating was hard for Brian because he was shy. To be a more impressive skater meant he would have to put more of his own personality into the skating, and for him that was quite difficult.

Nevertheless, Brian's great athletic ability allowed him to keep rising through the ranks of competitive skating. He came in second at the national championships in 1983, and qualified for the world championships. At the worlds, in Helsinki, Finland, Brian became the first skater to land six different triple jumps—the

Salchow, Lutz, Axel, toe loop, loop, and flip—in a long program in competition. But his lack of attention to his presentation prevented him from

RICHARD MACKSON/SPORTS ILLUSTRATED

finishing higher than seventh.

In 1984, Brian finished second at the national championships behind Scott Hamilton and qualified for the Olympics, which were being held that year in Sarajevo, Yugoslavia. In Sarajevo, Brian finished fifth. Scott Hamilton won the gold medal, and Brian's future archrival, Brian Orser of Canada, won the silver.

Through it all, Brian stayed with Linda Leaver as his coach. Top figure skaters usually change coaches many times during their careers, and Ms. Leaver was not very well known in skating circles. She had been a figure skater when she was young and began coaching to earn money while her husband attended graduate school at Stanford University, not far from Sunnyvale. "No one has ever come this far with a totally unknown coach," said Brian's mom in 1988. "I can't tell you how many times people in the skating community told Brian to get rid of her."

Linda Leaver understood Brian's style and what he was trying to do with his skating. She also understood her limits, and when she thought Brian needed help she couldn't provide, she and Brian would pack their bags and visit a coach who could help. Brian appreciated his coach's loyalty, and as he grew into an adult, the two became very close friends. It was with Ms. Leaver as his coach that Brian began his quest for an Olympic gold medal.

In 1985, Brian won the national championship for the first time. He did so by landing seven triple jumps in his free skating routine! It was the first of four consecutive national titles that he would win.

A shy person, Brian had to learn to put more personality into his skating.

The world championships, however, were more of a challenge. In 1985, he finished third, behind Soviet skater Alexandr Fadeev and Brain Orser. By the time the next year's world championships came around, Brian Boitano was 22 and a two-time national champion; he felt he had a good shot at winning the title. After a clean but dull short program, Brian was in fourth place. But his free skating program had such fire and style, as well as athleticism, that he pulled into first place and won his first world championship.

Brian Orser finished second, the place he had

held for the last three years. He had had enough; he was beginning to get a reputation for always coming in second. After the 1986 worlds, he consulted a sports psychologist to help him overcome any mental blocks that might be keeping him from being able to win.

The psychologist's help worked. The next year, 1987, Brian Orser came to Cincinnati, Ohio, and took away Brian Boitano's world championship. He skated a nearly flawless program, with six triple jumps including two triple Axels. Brian Boitano, who was always looking to try new jumps even if it meant risking a championship, had tried to become the first man ever to land a quadruple loop jump—four full turns in the air—in competition. And he had attempted it at the worlds. But as he came out of the "quad," as skaters call it, he fell and lost the world title.

"Life goes on," he said, not long after the loss. "I'll probably be a better skater for this happening."

That was exactly what happened. After his loss to the more artistic Orser, Brian decided that he needed to work more on his presentation than mastering difficult new moves if he hoped to beat out his rival for an Olympic gold medal.

So, Brian and Linda Leaver asked Sandra Bezic, a former Canadian pairs champion who had become a skating choreographer, for help. Sandra knew just what to do. "Artistically, a lot of people thought that Orser was superior to him and that my Brian just might not have it," Ms. Bezic said in 1988. "I was worried about that myself. But he does have it. He just needed some direction."

When Brian was choosing his own music, he usually skated to rock and roll or fiddle tunes, and he performed the role of a skating cowboy, just as Orser

Brian grew up in the shadow of the Golden Gate Bridge, in a town outside San Francisco called Sunnyvale.

HEINZ KLUETMEIER/SPORTS ILLUSTRATED

did. But Ms. Bezic wanted to get rid of the busy music and routines, and bring out the beauty of Brian's skating by using simple music. "He's powerful—and his jumps are incredible," she said. "I wanted to showcase simplicity instead of shtick."

For Brian's Olympic short program, Ms. Bezic chose *Les Patineurs* (French for "The Skaters"), a ballet about a boy who shows off his skating on a frozen pond while other skaters watch. In one part of the program, the choreographer had Brian do a triple Axel-double loop combination, and then wipe the "snow" off his skate blade, throwing it to the ice. It was supposed to be a cocky move—and one which didn't come easily to Brian.

For the long program, Ms. Bezic chose music from the movie *Napoleon*. (Napoleon Bonaparte was a 19th-century French emperor, notorious for waging war.) The music had a military sound to it, and Brian skated as though he were a soldier in Napoleon's army; he even wore a military outfit, which he and Ms. Leaver picked out.

"Brian always felt a little vulnerable on the ice," said Ms. Bezic. "With these two programs, either as the military man or the arrogant boy, he can hide behind a character. It gives him a mask. That helps when you're putting your heart and soul on the ice."

Brian practiced about six hours a day, and focused all of his attention on performing well in the Olympics. He wanted to win a gold medal, but most of all, he wanted to give his greatest performance at the Games. Brian always wanted the best from himself, and no less so in front of all the people who would be watching him on television in the United States.

When the 1988 Olympics began in Calgary, Canada, Brian was ready. He knew that Brian Orser would be tough competition, and the media went crazy talking and writing about what they called "The Battle of the Brians." He tried to block that out; he just wanted to skate well.

After the compulsories, which counted for 30 percent of the score, Brian Boitano was in second place; Brian Orser was in third. Alexandr Fadeev of the Soviet Union was first. But Alexandr fell during his short program, and his gold medal hopes were all but dashed. Brian Orser skated an energetic short program, while Brian Boitano skated more cautiously. Orser won the short program, and Boitano held on to a narrow lead.

It all came down to the long program. Brian Boitano was first up among the final group of six skaters. As he stepped onto the ice, Sandra Bezic whispered to him, "It's your moment, show them your soul."

When Brian began to skate, he was a combination of passion and perfection. Early in the program, he nailed his trademark, the 'Tano triple jump. The move is a triple Lutz with one arm over his head, and the other arm cradled in front as if holding a dance partner. Then he landed a triple Axel-double toe loop combination. That was followed by a camel spin so perfect that someone could have balanced a stack of books on his back. He even landed the most difficult move in his program, a triple flip-triple toe loop combination, and made the audience gasp when he leaned back so far in his graceful spread eagle that it looked as though

he would surely fall. In a final flourish, he performed a double Axel and finished with a triumphant smile.

There was no doubt in anyone's mind that this had been Brian's best performance ever. He had skated with such ease, he said, that "it felt like angels were lifting me and spinning me." His scores were high, but not so high that Orser couldn't beat them.

Brian Orser also skated to military-style music. He needed a perfect program to beat Brian Boitano, and he thought he could do it. But seconds into his program, he wobbled as he came out of a triple jump. At the end, he did a double Axel instead of a scheduled triple. But it was a good program and he received high scores, including one perfect 6.0 for artistic impression. When all the scores were tallied up, though, five of the nine judges had placed Brian Boitano first. He had won the gold medal. Even better, he had given the performance of a lifetime. "I would have hated to win the gold medal," he said, "with anything but my best."

A month later, at the world championships in Budapest, Hungary, Brian won another gold and landed his quadruple jump. But he wasn't the first to do that jump. Only a few minutes before, Kurt Browning of Canada became the first man to land a "quad" in competition.

After the worlds, Brian retired and turned pro. He began to skate in ice shows and television shows, often with the 1988 women's gold medal winner, Katarina Witt. In 1989, Brian and Katarina made a skating movie together, called *Carmen on Ice*, and they skated together in Brian's own touring ice show, called *Skating*.

Brian never lost his desire to skate daring technical programs, though. "It's not like once you win the Olympics your job is over, you're the champ, and you can just go out there and float around and smile," Brian said recently. "You can't do that. You've got to be an athlete." Brian Boitano couldn't skate any other way.

CHAPTER 13

Katarina Witt

She could really wow the crowds with her charm, beauty, and skating ability

HEINZ KLUETMEIER/SPORTS ILLUSTRATED

Katarina Witt [*vit*] was such an entertaining performer that it was easy to forget she was an athlete. It was particularly easy for men to forget. After she won a gold medal at the 1984 Olympics, Katarina received 35,000 fan letters, many of which were marriage proposals from men she had never met. A *Sports Illustrated* writer, who met her in 1986, described Katarina simply as "so fresh-faced, so blue-eyed, so ruby lipped, so 12-car pile-up gorgeous."

There was no denying that Katarina used her beauty, along with a generous helping of charm, to enhance her skating performance. But neither would have mattered a bit if Katarina hadn't been such a good skater. Her performances were as technically flawless as they were alluring. She made the skating and the charm look easy—but both were the products of years of hard work.

Katarina was born on December 3, 1965, and grew up in Karl-Marx-Stadt, a city in what was then

East Germany, not far from the Czechoslovakian border. East Germany and West Germany were separate countries from 1949 until 1990, as a result of World War II. The two countries are now reunited, but Katarina grew up under the Communist government of

> **A**though Katarina made skating and charming an audience look easy, they were the results of years of hard work.

East Germany.

Karl-Marx-Stadt was a industrial, unglamorous place. Katarina's father, Manfred, was a departmental director at a plant-and-seed cooperative. Her mother, Käthe, was a physical therapist.

The family, which also included Katarina's brother Axel, lived near the Küchwald ice skating rink and, when Katarina was 5, she begged her mother to let her try skating. Her mother, who would have preferred she try dance, signed her up for group lessons. Katarina joined the class about halfway through the year. "The teacher said I would have to learn as much in half a year as the others learned in a year," Katarina said. "I did that."

When Katarina was 10, she was discovered by a woman named Jutta Mueller [*YUTE-a MULE-er*], who coached at the Küchwald rink, and was the best known figure skating coach in East Germany. Frau (Frau means "Mrs." in German) Mueller's pupils had included the 1968 Olympic silver medalist Gabriele Seyfert, who was her daughter from her first marriage. "When Frau Mueller took me, I was too young to realize the great thing that had happened to me," Katarina said. "If Frau Mueller takes a girl or a boy, it's because she sees them as a champion sometime."

In many Communist countries, athletes are typically picked out by important coaches and trainers at a very young age and taught to become champions. The government provides these children with extensive coaching and privileges that are not available to ordinary citizens. Katarina was chosen to be one of those future champions.

Katarina began to skate with Frau Mueller six hours a day, 11 months out of the year. Her schedule at a special sports school was arranged so that she could spend most of the day on the ice. "I would never have been a skater in another country," Katarina said, "because my parents could not have afforded it."

Frau Mueller was a very demanding coach. She expected Katarina to practice until she reached perfection. "People have a natural tendency to seek comfort," Frau Mueller once said, "and that doesn't work if you want to get to the top in this sport. I always have to prod my students."

Frau Mueller taught Katarina how to perform jumps and spins, chose Katarina's music and costumes, and choreographed her free skating programs. She also taught her how to captivate judges and an audience. Frau Mueller taught Katarina how to apply makeup, fix her hair, smile, and make eye contact. Frau Mueller knew that skating judges rate an athlete's appearance as well as their performance, and she made sure her students always looked as though they had just stepped out of a beauty salon.

Frau Mueller had a special system for teaching her students. "I try to put younger skaters alongside the older ones," she said. When Katarina was 12, she was already working with Anett Pötzsch, who would become a two-time world champion and Olympic gold medalist. "By the time Anett was world champion," said Mueller, "Katarina was already training at her side." Katarina still spends time with Anett; Anett married Katarina's brother in 1984.

In 1982, Katarina became the East German champion. That same year, she came in second to Elaine Zayak of the United States in the world championships. The next year, Katarina won the East German championships again and became the new European champion.

Katarina caused quite a fuss at the European championships that year. She often liked to create characters, as ballerinas do, in her skating routines. At the 1983 Europeans, she was skating to the music of Wolfgang Mozart, the 18th-century Austrian composer, and she wanted to wear knickers, as Mozart had in the style of his day. The staid judges threatened to penalize Katarina if she didn't wear a skirt, which she eventually did. But just to make the judges mad, Frau Mueller showed up at the rink the next day wearing knickers!

By 1984, 18-year-old Katarina was considered to have a chance at winning the Olympic gold medal, even though she had not won the worlds. Because she had won the European championship that year, she qualified to compete in the Winter Games, which were being held in Sarajevo, Yugoslavia.

Two American women, Rosalyn Sumners and

MANNY MILLAN/SPORTS ILLUSTRATED

Katarina loved to create characters when she skated. For her 1988 Olympic program, she was Carmen.

Elaine Zayak, were the favorites going into the Olympics. But after the compulsories and the short program, Katarina was in first place, Rosalyn was in second, and Elaine had dropped out of contention into 13th place. So the free skating program turned into a showdown between Katarina and Rosalyn for the gold medal.

Katarina skated before Rosalyn to a medley of American show tunes, including "I've Got Rhythm" and "Embraceable You." She took to the ice in a smashing red sequined dress, and skated as beautifully as she looked. She soared off the ice in the three triple jumps she included and landed effortlessly. Her performance drew 11 5.8's, five 5.9's and two 5.7's from the judges.

Rosalyn skated next, knowing that she would have to go all out to win. Her skating was technically perfect, but conservative and without its usual fire. She turned one of her triple jumps into a double, and one of her double jumps into a single near the end of her program—and lost the gold by only a 10th of a point. Katarina had become the new Olympic champion.

Several weeks later, Katarina traveled to Ottawa, Canada, to compete in the world championships—and she won that, too. It was when she arrived back home after her trip that she discovered that she had received all those fan letters. There were so many that she had no place to store them so she put them in her bathtub. Frau Mueller's charm lessons had worked.

Katarina won the world championship again in 1985 in Tokyo and then began thinking about retiring. She was tired of all the practicing and how it took up so many hours that she had no time for other things she wanted to do.

However, if Katarina needed extra motivation to continue skating, she got it the next year, at the 1986 world championships in Geneva, Switzerland. Katarina was in third place after the compulsories, but she fell in her short program while attempting a double loop jump and dropped to fourth place. U.S. champion Debi Thomas moved into first place.

Katarina saw her world championship slipping away, and she was determined to keep it. Katarina may have been all smiles and fluttering eyelashes on the outside, but inside she was a steely competitor who hated to lose. In her long program, she skated to the music of *West Side Story*, pretending she was the story's heroine, Maria. Katarina knew she had to skate perfectly in her long program, and she did. Two judges awarded her perfect scores of 6.0—the first 6.0's that Katarina had ever earned in international competition.

Still, the scores were not enough to beat Debi Thomas, who became the new world champion. Katarina immediately put aside any thoughts of retirement. "I have decided I will continue skating," Katarina told reporters afterward, "until I get the title back."

The next year, the world championships were held in Cincinnati, Ohio. The people of Cincinnati fell in love with Katarina, who is called Kati [*KAH-dee*] by her friends. When they were permitted, they crammed into the arena just to watch her practice. Debi Thomas's coach, Alex McGowan, accused Katarina of "milking the crowd" when she acknowledged the crowd's clapping with waves and smiles. Mr. McGowan said that her friendliness was "planned, not spontaneous."

That was partly true. As part of her coaching, Frau Mueller had taught Katarina to pick one man out of the audience while she was skating and play to him, as if she were dying to sit by his side as soon as the performance was over. "A skater does not skate for herself," said Frau Mueller. "She should please the crowd."

In Cincinnati, Katarina pleased the crowd and the judges. She repeated her *West Side Story* routine from the previous year's world championships. Skating after Debi, Katarina knew she couldn't falter. She skated beautifully and hit her five triple jumps and two double Axels perfectly. Seven of the nine judges placed her first, and she regained her world championship.

Now that Katarina had won back her title, she began preparing to win her second gold medal at the

1988 Winter Olympics in Calgary, Canada. No woman since Sonja Henie had won two gold medals. Sonja actually had won three—in 1928, 1932, and 1936. But Katarina thought she could do it. "I worked harder on this than I ever have," she told a reporter before the Olympic competition began. "In the last four years there has been just sports for me. This was the most important thing." That meant sacrifices, such as no ice cream (which Katarina adores), no staying out late at night, and no boyfriend.

Katarina chose for her Olympic free skating program to skate to the music of Georges Bizet's *Carmen,* an opera about a Spanish gypsy who is killed by her jealous lover. Oddly enough, Debi Thomas had chosen the same music. The media loved this; they billed Katarina and Debi as the "Dueling Carmens."

Debi had been the only skater to beat Katarina since 1984, and now was the one most likely to upset Katarina's gold medal dreams. Before the Olympics began, Debi pointed out one difference between their programs, which she hoped was a sign: "Katarina dies at the end of hers," she said, "and I don't."

Debi was leading Katarina after the compulsories and short program. Katarina had one shot left at moving ahead. On the night of the free skating, Katarina performed before Debi. Kati appeared on the ice in a low-cut red costume, adorned with beads and ruffles. She was a dramatic, flirting Carmen, but her skating was conservative. Katarina didn't want to make a mistake, so near the end of the program she turned a triple jump into a double jump. Her program was not as exciting as

usual, but she made no mistakes. And to top it off, she finished with a flair—laying outstretched on the ice, in a pose of death.

Katarina's scores were low for her: she received mostly 5.6's to 5.8's for technical merit and 5.8's and 5.9's for artistic impression. She wondered if her scores would be high enough to win.

But Katarina didn't have to wonder for long. Debi landed poorly from a triple jump early on, and nearly fell out of another triple. With those mistakes, Debi all but handed the gold medal to her rival.

Katarina won the gold medal, and Debi won the bronze. Elizabeth Manley of Canada, who had actually placed first in the free skating program, took the silver. A month later, Katarina went to Budapest, Hungary, and successfully defended her world championship. Then—with four world championships and two Olympic gold medals—Katarina turned professional.

Now Katarina skates throughout Europe and the United States, often with her good friend Brian Boitano, who won the men's gold medal in Calgary. She also has had time to have a boyfriend.

While she misses the thrill of competition, Katarina is still doing what she loves most: performing. Even though she could always do all the difficult jumps of figure skating, performing before an audience is what always brought out the best skating in Katarina Witt.

"Kati skates for the crowds," an East German friend once told *Sports Illustrated.* "She cannot imagine life without an audience."

Katarina became the first woman singles skater since Sonja Henie to win two gold medals.

MANNY MILLAN/SPORTS ILLUSTRATED

CHAPTER 14

Debi Thomas

She refused to give up the rest of her life for skating, and still became a champion

Debi Thomas liked to do things *her* way. In the sometimes stuffy circles of elite figure skating, she was a refreshing change. Even though she had an enormous talent, Debi refused to give up her education and her social life to focus on becoming a great skater. Nonetheless, she did become a good skater and, in 1986, she won the world championship.

Once, Debi tried to follow a traditional figure skating path. When she was 13 years old, in 1980, she left school so she would have more time to train, and studied by taking correspondence courses at home. She thought that she could become the national junior champion that year, but all her practicing yielded only disappointment: Debi didn't even make it to the sectional tournament.

"Right then," Debi later told *Time* magazine, "I decided that I wasn't going to put the rest of my life on the line in front of some panel of judges who just might not like my yellow dress." Debi started skating because it was fun. When Debi was 3½ years old, her mother had taken her to the Ice Follies, where

Debi saw the Follies' Mr. Frick, the rubber-legged skating clown. Debi wanted to have that much fun on the ice.

Debi began to take group skating lessons when she was 5 years old. At the time, she lived with her mom and her older half-brother Rick in San Jose, California, a city about 30 miles south of San Francisco. Her mother was a computer programming analyst; her parents had divorced when Debi was very young. Debi's father, McKinley Thomas, also lived in Northern California and worked in the computer industry.

Debi entered and won her first competition, at her skating club, when she was 9 years old. When she was 10, she began to train under coach Alex McGowan, from Scotland, at the Redwood City Ice Lodge, halfway between San Josc and San Francisco.

Debi was very advanced for her age. She landed her first triple jump when she was 11. When she was 12, she advanced to the national finals in the novice

To prepare for the 1988 Olympics, Debi picked up some pointers from the famous ballet dancer, Mikhail Baryshnikov.

BILL EPPRIDGE/SPORTS ILLUSTRATED

class and won a silver medal. It was after that finish that Debi decided to leave school for a while to concentrate on skating.

When Debi returned to school, she enrolled in San Mateo High, which was farther from her San Jose home but closer to the Redwood City Ice Lodge. For four years, Debi's mom drove about 150 miles a day, dropping Debi off at school before work, returning to take her to practice, and then picking her up again after working late. Debi practiced six hours a day, six days a week—except, of course, when she had to take time off to study for a test.

Debi and her mom had to make financial sacrifices for Debi's skating. It cost as much as $25,000 a year, and money was always tight. Debi's mom, her dad, her grandparents, and even her half-brother chipped in. But Debi usually stopped skating during the summer while her mom caught up on bills. Debi also skated in second-hand skates, and sewed many of her own skating costumes.

Despite those obstacles, Debi continued to gain valuable experience at the highest levels of the sport, and soon that began to pay off. In 1985, two months before her 18th birthday, Debi came in second at the national championships and then

HEINZ KLUETMEIER/SPORTS ILLUSTRATED

finished fifth at the world championships. That summer she also won her first major competition, the National Sports Festival (now called the Olympic Festival), which is a U.S. competition in the Olympic sports. From 1983 to 1985, Debi moved from being 13th among all U.S. women's figure skaters to number 2, just behind U.S. champion Tiffany Chin.

But Debi wasn't satisfied just with being a top skater. In the fall of 1986, she enrolled at Stanford University, one of the nation's top schools, and chose medical microbiology as her major. Debi wanted to become an orthopedic surgeon (a bone doctor). "A lot of people think it'll be too difficult to train and go to school full time," Debi once said, "but I think it'll help me from frying my brain. You have to be dedicated to be a skater, but you can really wreck yourself by thinking 'skating, skating, skating.'"

Debi's coach, Mr. McGowan, was worried that going to school would hurt Debi's skating career. He was particularly concerned in 1986, when Debi was a Stanford freshman, and the national championships, in New York, were coming up in February. Debi had only trained for five weeks.

After her disappointing bronze medal finish in the Olympics, Debi planned to attend medical school.

Debi said she was hoping for a "little miracle," and she got it. She performed five triple jumps in her long program—an extraordinary feat in women's skating—and upset Tiffany Chin. Debi had become the new national champion!

Six months later, Debi pulled off an even more astounding upset. At the world championships in Geneva, Switzerland, Debi was skating against Katarina Witt, the 1984 and 1985 world champion. Debi was sure she could beat her. "Katarina does the stuff, and smiles," Debi told *Sports Illustrated*, "but her jumps aren't all that high."

Katarina's jumps proved to be her downfall in Geneva. During the short program, she was attempting a double loop jump when she crashed into the boards along the ice. Debi, who had won the short program, was now in a position to win. In her long program, she landed four triple jumps, including one breathtaking triple-double jump combination, and won the world championship. In doing so, Debi also made history. She became the first black woman ever to win a world championship in singles figure skating.

But Debi would not keep her titles for long. Because she was studying so much at Stanford, she didn't begin serious training for the 1987 national championships until five weeks before they were to begin. Then she pulled the calf muscles in *both* of her legs, and couldn't practice for a week. She tried to come back too soon and developed tendinitis in both ankles. (Tendinitis is a soreness in the tendon, which is the tissue that connects a muscle with the rest of the body.) When Debi arrived in Tacoma, Washington, for the nationals, she was in pain.

Still, when the competition began, Debi was able to build up a comfortable lead in the compulsories and the short program. But she missed her first jump in the long program and lost her national crown to Jill Trenary, a skater from Minnesota.

A month later, Debi lost the world championships in Cincinnati, Ohio, to Katarina Witt. Debi had won the compulsory figures, and even though she was injured, she performed an athletic, jazzy long program. Alas, neither were enough to overcome a poor performance in her short program. Debi had missed one of the required moves, a dou-

Debi's trademark was a high-energy, athletic program; in winning the 1986 world title she landed four triple jumps.

STEVE POWELL/SPORTS ILLUSTRATED

ble Axel, and finished back in seventh place.

Debi's coach blamed her lack of training. "If she trained as much as other skaters, she'd be almost unbeatable," Mr. McGowan said. He convinced Debi to take the 1987-88 school year off from Stanford in order to train for the Olympics. His ice rink in Redwood City had closed because of financial difficulties, so he and Debi moved to Boulder, Colorado, to train for a few months at the University of Colorado's rink.

Debi realized that if she was going to win the gold medal, she would have to beat Katarina Witt at her own game. Katarina was considered the more artistic of the two skaters, while Debi was the more powerful and athletic. Debi enlisted the help of Mikhail Baryshnikov, a famous ballet dancer who was also the director of the American Ballet Theater (ABT) in New York City. He worked briefly with Debi and then sent George de la Peña, one of ABT's former dancers and choreographers, to Boulder. There, Mr. de la Peña taught Debi how to hold her arms and her head like a ballerina, and also how to appear more moved by the music. "George has gotten me to open up on the ice, rather than just going from jump to jump to jump," Debi said at the time. "He worked a miracle with me."

In January of 1988, Debi warmed up for the Olympics by winning the national championship in Denver, regaining the title from Jill Trenary. A month later, she was in Calgary for the Olympics. Debi was the only woman who had beaten Katarina since 1984—and she was the only one who seemed to have any chance of upsetting her now. Debi had practiced more for the Olympics than she had for any competition in her life. All the preparation, however, seemed to backfire on her. She was not keeping the delicate balance between school and skating which had kept her sane. By the time she reached Calgary, she was tired of skating. "I do better when I am not as prepared," Debi said.

At first, Debi's burnout didn't show. She placed second in the compulsory figures, behind Kira Ivanova of the Soviet Union, but ahead of Katarina. Debi skated her short program flawlessly, "hitting every jump and engaging the audience with her megawatt smile," according to *Time* magazine. Even though many people thought that Debi's short program was better than Katarina's, the judges placed Katarina first.

After a second place finish in the short program, Debi went into the final phase of the competition in first place. Now, all she had to do was nail her free skating program. Months earlier, Debi had selected music from the opera *Carmen,* by Georges Bizet, for her long program. Unknown to her, it was the same music that Katarina had chosen for her long program. The music was passionate, and Debi wanted her skating to be passionate as well. She planned to open her routine with a daring triple jump-triple jump combination within the first 15 seconds. This is a very difficult combination to pull off, with no time to wind down from the first jump or to prepare for the second.

Katarina skated before Debi. Her Carmen was passionate, and her program was flawless, but it was conservative. That gave Debi a good chance. Debi, skating in a sequined black dress, needed to land her triple-triple combination early in the program to wow the judges and beat Katarina. But she mistakenly touched down with two feet on the second triple. It was a small error that wouldn't hurt her scores, but because it was a mistake, it drained her of all her hope.

"My heart wasn't in it after the first combination jump," she said later. "I tried as hard as I could, but when I didn't hit it, it was hard for me to keep going. I didn't want to be out there anymore."

Debi finished her program, almost missing one triple jump, then another, but still kept from falling. As she skated off the ice, she said to her coach, "I'm sorry." Neither Debi nor Katarina won the long program that night. That honor went to Elizabeth Manley, an energetic skater from Canada. Because the long program counted for 50 percent of the total score, Elizabeth moved into second place overall and won the silver medal. Katarina won the gold and Debi the bronze.

Debi was bitterly disappointed by that result. "The three weeks after the Olympics were probably the hardest of my life," she told *Sports Illustrated.* "I cried every day."

A month after the Olympics, Debi competed in the world championships in Budapest, Hungary, and again came away with a bronze. In Budapest, though, Debi revealed a bit of happy news: Between the Olympics and the worlds, she had married Brian Vanden Hogen, a University of Colorado student whom she had met while training in Boulder.

Soon after the world championships, Debi retired from amateur skating. She continues to skate as a professional—on the weekends. She graduated from Stanford in June of 1991, and took time off before starting medical school.

Debi's priorities never changed: Though she loved figure skating and excelled at it, she always knew that her education came first. That knowledge made her loss at the 1988 Olympics easier to accept. "You can't look at skating and feel that it's the only accomplishment in your life," she said in 1989. "It's just not enough."

Pairs Skating

Pairs skating first appeared as a competitive event in Vienna, Austria, in the late 1880s. Vienna was known for its love of music, and it was there that Jackson Haines first introduced skating to music, and that "dancing" on ice first became popular.

In the early days of pairs skating, partners were often of the same sex. The combination we now know, a man and a woman, was called "mixed pairs." This proved to be the most popular combination and, for the most part, the others faded away.

Pairs skating became an Olympic sport at the 1908 Games in London. And like singles, pairs has undergone an evolution of style over the years. In the first half of the 20th century, pairs skating became less like dancing and more acrobatic. Then in the 1960s, the Russian team of Oleg Protopopov and Lyudmila Belousova brought grace and beauty back to the event. Following them, Irina Rodnina, with her first partner, Aleksei Ulanov, and later with Alexandr Zaitsev, managed to combine both athletics and grace in the sport.

In the early days, pairs skaters were judged only on their free skating program. Then in the 1960s, the compulsory moves section, which is similar to the singles short program, was introduced. Today the compulsory moves section is worth 25 percent of the total score, and the free skating program is worth 75 percent.

Irina Rodnina and Aleksei Ulanov were masters of the chemistry that makes pairs skating beautiful.

T. TANUMA/SPORTS ILLUSTRATED

Ice dancing is the newest figure skating event to join the Olympic roster. In ice dancing, the skating pair must follow rules that limit the jumps and lifts they can use and regulate the amount of time they can skate apart from each other.

Even though it started at about the same time as pairs, ice dancing wasn't included in world championship competition until 1952, and it didn't become an Olympic sport until 1976. Ice dancing's popularity reached new heights in 1984, when the British team of Jayne Torvill and Christopher Dean won the Olympic gold medal. Torvill and Dean brought to ice dancing an elegance and imagination that redefined the event.

CHAPTER 15

The Protopopovs

Their desire to stress artistry instead of acrobatics revolutionized pairs skating

To Oleg Protopopov and his wife, Lyudmila Belousova, skating was always an art. The Russian couple, who became the first figure skaters from the Soviet Union ever to win an Olympic gold medal, saw skating as a way to express the love between them. "Art cannot be measured by points," Oleg told reporters in 1968, after they had won their second gold medal. "We skate from the heart. To us it is spiritual beauty that matters. . . . These pairs of brother and sister, how can they convey the emotion, the love that exists between a man and a woman? That is what we try to show."

The Protopopovs changed the sport of pairs skating. Before them, pairs skating was very athletic, with couples performing ever more difficult lifts and jumps. Skaters basically skated from one "trick"—a lift or a jump—to another. They mastered the difficult technical moves, but ignored the artistry needed to express the music and convey the chemistry between them. The Protopopovs were more like dancers who were performing a romantic ballet.

Oleg had learned about the beauty of moving to music from his mother, who had been a ballerina. Oleg grew up in Leningrad, the city in northwestern Russia which was, and still is, home to many of the Soviet Union's leading dancers, painters, writers, and musicians.

The Leningrad that Oleg grew up in, however, was one disrupted by war. Oleg was 9 years old in 1941, during World War II, when German soldiers invaded Leningrad and took control of the city. The Germans gave up the city early in 1944, but during the war-time occupation, the people of Leningrad experienced terror, shortages, and starvation.

In spite of the war, Oleg taught himself to skate. There were no skating rinks open, so Oleg, like other children, skated by being towed behind vehicles on the frozen streets of Leningrad. The night

JERRY COOKE/SPORTS ILLUSTRATED

In black tuxedo and simple dress, Oleg and Ludmilla looked like a couple performing a romantic ballet.

after the war ended, Oleg joined a local sports club, where he was able to skate on a rink.

In 1949, when he was 17, Oleg finished second in the Russian youth championships. Two years later, he joined the Soviet navy, but continued to skate. In 1953, he placed third in the Russian pairs championship, with partner Margarita Bogoyavlenskaya [*bo-go-ya-VLEN-sky-ah*]. The Navy was so impressed by his performance that it decided to give Oleg time off every week to train at a rink in Moscow.

It was at that rink, in 1954, that Oleg met 18-

year-old Lyudmila Belousova. Lyudmila had begun skating when she was 16, after being inspired by a Sonja Henie film called *Sun Valley Serenade*.

Oleg and Lyudmila met, literally, by bumping into one another. "The rink was so small, it was hard not to bump into each other," Oleg told a reporter for *The Christian Science Monitor*. "So we held hands and began spinning around together just for the fun of it. This chance spinning was the beginning of a new era for us both."

Oleg and Lyudmila became partners, and only a few months later, they placed third in the U.S.S.R.'s national pairs competition. They also fell in love. In 1957, they were married.

The Protopopovs competed in their first Olympics in 1960, in Squaw Valley, California. They placed ninth, and Dick Button recalls that their performance was awful. "It reminded me of watching Peggy Fleming compete for the first time," Dick said. "They were untutored, untrained colts."

The Protopopovs had no mentor to teach them and no one to look to as examples. They needed more skating experience. The next year, they won the Soviet pairs championship, the first of eight national titles they would win. They were hoping to become world champions that year, as well. Because of the plane crash that killed the entire U.S. skating team, however, the 1961 world competition, to be held in Prague, Czechoslovakia, was canceled.

For the next two years the Protopopovs would come frustratingly close to winning the world championship. In 1962, they finished second to Maria and Otto Jelinek of Canada. Then, in 1963, they were runners-up to Marika Kilius and Hans Jurgen Baumler, a West German team. Hans and Marika relied on acrobatics much more than the Protopopovs, who were already becoming famous for their graceful style.

The 1963 world championships set the stage for the Olympics a year later in Innsbruck, Austria. There, many international skating fans saw the Protopopovs perform for the first time.

Although neither Oleg nor his thin, blonde wife were particularly good-looking, together they created beauty. At 5'9",

Oleg was six inches taller than Lyudmila, but they fit perfectly together. While their West German rivals dressed and fussed over themselves like movie stars, the Protopopovs stressed simplicity in their skating and in their appearance—Oleg usually skated in a black tuxedo and Lyudmila in a single-colored, unadorned dress.

In the Olympic free skating program, Hans and Marika skated before the Protopopovs.

The West Germans' routine was filled with tricky lifts and jumps.

The Protopopovs performed few lifts, preferring to emphasize the beauty of a man and a woman skating together.

The Protopopovs, by comparison, skated a much simpler program. They used classical music, and the overall impression they left was one of dancing, not athletics. They moved like shadows and flowed over the ice as if floating on air. While the West Germans had included 14 lifts in their program, the Protopopovs included only six.

But this time, the judges approved of the Protopopovs' style; five of the nine judges placed the Protopopovs first. They won the gold medal; they were the first Soviets ever to win an Olympic figure skating event.

The Protopopovs had beaten the West Germans by less than one point. Hans and Marika were convinced that *they* deserved the gold medal, not the Protopopovs. "We say skating should be sport, not ballet," Hans complained to a reporter. "But you see that sport no longer wins at the Olympics." As it turned out, Hans and Marika were later stripped of their silver medal when it was discovered that they had appeared in a professional ice show before the Olympics.

In 1965, the Protopopovs won their

JERRY COOKE/SPORTS ILLUSTRATED

first world championship. They dominated their sport through the 1968 Olympics, and they began a Soviet domination of pairs skating that would last for many years.

"The Protopopovs were the opposite pole from skaters who rely on strength and power," Dick Button once said. "What they concentrated on was unison, two people skating as one. They did not allow the other elements (such as acrobatics) to intrude on their performances. What they created was a choreographic whole."

Although they are remembered primarily for their grace and elegance, they are known in skating circles for creating three new versions of the death spiral.

L ike all of the g r e a t skaters, the Protopopovs achieved their grace through long hours of practice. And practices were not always fun. Oleg was both partner and coach. He was a stern perfectionist, who ran practices with the discipline of a military officer. Lyudmila did not seem to mind. She agreed with Oleg's goals.

During practices, Lyudmila wore a 22-pound belt around her waist. "We call it 22 pounds of grace," Oleg told a reporter from *The Christian Science Monitor*. "Then when she takes it off [for a competition] she feels as weightless as an astronaut and can skate and jump that much better!"

By 1968, the Protopopovs had won three world championships. Their success was remarkable, especially considering that they were a good 10 years older than most of their competition. When the 1968 Olympics were held in Grenoble, France, Oleg was 35 and Lyudmila, 32. Despite their ages, they were heavily favored to win another gold medal.

In the free skating program in Grenoble, Oleg and Lyudmila skated one of the finest performances of their careers. They highlighted romance and nationalism by skating, as usual, to the music of some

From 1963 to 1968, Oleg and Ludmilla dominated pairs, winning two gold medals and three world titles.

of the great classical Russian composers— Rachmaninoff [*rook-MON-nin-off*], Tchaikovsky [*chye-KOFF-ski*], and Shostakovich [*sha-sta-KO-vich*].

The first half of

JERRY COOKE/SPORTS ILLUSTRATED

the program was slow and balletic, and the Protopopovs often gazed into one another's eyes as if they were the only people in the Olympic stadium. In this part of the program, they included a great deal of "shadow skating," which means that they performed the same movements while skating close together. About a minute into the program, Oleg dipped Lyudmila as if they were skating the tango, and they glided across the ice in a romantic dip position.

They began to pick up speed after Oleg lifted Lyudmila high above his head, holding both of her hands while she assumed the spread-eagle position, a lift known as the lasso. Then they thrilled the audience with one of the purest moves of all; side by side, as if they were one skater, they traced two large circles on the ice in an arabesque position.

Near the end, the Protopopovs made an uncharacteristic mistake. Oleg launched Lyudmila into a double twist lift, in which she spun around twice in the air before he caught her and returned her to the ice. However, upon landing, Lyudmila momentarily lost her balance and wobbled. But even with that, their performance was considered by many to be one of the most beautiful in amateur pairs skating.

The Protopopovs won the gold medal again, although once more by a narrow margin. Other skaters had noticed that the Protopopovs' balletic style was rewarded by the judges, and they too were moving in that direction. The Soviet team of Tatiana Zhuk and Aleksandr Gorelik, who were much younger, finished less than three points behind the Protopopovs. The Protopopovs didn't mind that the finish was so close; they were exhilarated by competition. Speaking in English, Oleg said: "They [Zhuk and Gorelik] helped us to go up. If there are no good competitors, you don't grow up."

By winning the 1968 gold medal, Oleg and Lyudmila had become only the second couple to win the Olympic pairs competition twice. French skaters Andrée and Pierre Brunet, who went on to coach Carol Heiss, won the pairs in 1928 and 1932.

A few weeks after the Olympics, the Protopopovs won their fourth world championship, in Geneva, Switzerland. Then they returned to Leningrad, and continued to practice as much as they ever had; they had no plans to retire. When a reporter asked whether the Protopopovs would consider working as coaches, Oleg shook his head no. "I can only say," he told the reporter, "that any great painter who loves his art will stay with it."

As much as the Protopopovs wished to continue competing, though, their era was over. In 1969, they were beaten at the European championships, which they had won four times, by the younger Soviet team of Irina Rodnina and Aleksei Ulanov. At the world championships in Colorado Springs, Colorado, later that year, the Protopopovs finished third. Again, Irina and Aleksei, who would become the 1972 Olympic champions, won the title. The following year, the Protopopovs did not even make the Soviet team. Reluctantly, they turned professional and began to skate with a troupe in their hometown of Leningrad.

The government of the Soviet Union had showered the Protopopovs with honors and special privileges during their amateur years. They were given an apartment, a car, and travel opportunities. In the late 1970s, however, Oleg had a falling out with Soviet skating officials. They reportedly insisted that Oleg stop performing and become a coach for younger Soviet skaters. Oleg—who saw himself as an artist, not a coach—refused.

In 1979, while on tour in Switzerland, Oleg and Lyudmila defected from the Soviet Union. They asked the Swiss government if they could stay and live in Switzerland—without the Soviet government's permission—and the Swiss said yes. Skating fans around the world were stunned by their defection, as were the Soviets. "For athletes of their caliber, there are no problems," said a Soviet sports official. "They had everything they wanted here."

But they didn't have what they desired most: artistic freedom. They preferred to leave their comfortable lives rather than to have someone chart their career paths for them. Shortly after defecting, they signed a three-year contract to skate with the Ice Capades. Since then, they have been frequent visitors to the U.S., and have been guest coaches for the University of Maryland's summer figure skating program.

The Protopopovs still see themselves as artists, and they are staying true to their vision.

CHAPTER 16

Irina Rodnina and Partners

With two partners, through joy and sorrow, Irina ruled her sport

When Irina Rodnina won her first Olympic gold medal in 1972, her heart was filled with sorrow. She and her partner, Aleksei Ulanov, who were both from the Soviet Union, had narrowly beaten their Soviet rivals, Lyudmila Smirnova and Andrei Suraikin. But instead of bursting into a smile after her winning performance, 22-year-old Irina burst into tears.

It seemed that while she and Aleksei were the picture of harmony on the ice, off the ice, they were barely speaking. Aleksei had fallen in love with Lyudmila Smirnova, and Irina's heart was broken. Irina and Aleksei had won three world championships as a team, but Irina knew that after this season they would never skate together again.

As soon as Aleksei returned to the Soviet Union, he and Lyudmila were married. However, before they would become skating partners, too, Aleksei had to skate in one last world championship with Irina.

At the world championships in Calgary, Canada, the tension be-

*I*rina, here with Aleksei, was known as the Ice Devil for her fiery and athletic style.

T. TANUMA/SPORTS ILLUSTRATED

tween Aleksei and Irina showed: During a practice session, he dropped Irina on her head and she had to spend the night in the hospital. But she recovered, and in their final performance together, they won a fourth world championship.

When Irina returned to her home in Moscow, she was devastated. "I put myself into bed and didn't want to skate anymore," she wrote in her autobiography *Uneven Ice*. "I was really determined to quit figure skating." But Irina had not come so far as an athlete by being a quitter. Before long, she was at the rink again—and looking for a new partner.

Irina's willingness to keep going after terrible heartbreak was just one example of her toughness. As a figure skater, Irina was known as the Ice Devil. Her skating was fiery and athletic and, almost always, flawless. She was an emotional woman, and she displayed a drive for perfection that is seen only in athletes at the highest level of sport. And that is where Irina stood—at the highest level.

Even as a child, Irina was tough. She was born on September 12, 1949, in Moscow. When she was very young, she was stricken with tuberculosis, an infectious disease that usually affects the lungs and can be fatal. Irina learned how to skate because her parents wanted her to play outside in the fresh air. In those days, people who had recovered from a bout of tuberculosis were urged to get as much fresh air as possible.

By the time she was 9, Irina was talented enough to be chosen to attend a special Children's Sports School. Under the Communist government of the Soviet Union, potential champions were selected at a very young age to receive special training. All of Irina's education—including her skating lessons and coaching—were paid for by the government.

At the Children's Sports School, Irina began to train under Stanislav Zhuk, a famous Soviet skating coach. When she was 15, she began to compete as a singles skater. Because she was small—just 4'11"—and easy to lift, she was moved into pairs skating the next year, and teamed with Aleksei. They were perfect for one another: Aleksei was considerably taller and quite strong. They skated together, practicing

five days a week for as much as seven hours a day. And they fell in love.

The training was very difficult. In her autobiography, Irina says of her coach: "From the first second of training, he chased us and himself all over the ice. . . . He didn't have enough with three hours of training, but then eight hours weren't enough for him either."

Irina and Aleksei began to excel in competition, but they skated in the shadow of the first great Soviet pairs team, Lyudmila Belousova and her husband, Oleg Protopopov. The Protopopovs had won the 1964 and 1968 Olympics.

Irina and Aleksei, along with their coach, knew that the only way that they could beat the older couple was by developing their own, very different style. The Protopopovs were graceful, artistic skaters; Irina and her partner became dynamic, acrobatic skaters.

After Alexei, her first partner, left her heartbroken, Irina fell in love with and married Sasha, her second partner.

The strategy worked. In 1969, in Colorado Springs, Colorado, Irina and Aleksei became the new world champions. Their victory was a surprise because figure skating judges rarely give championships to newcomers. Sadly, though, that world championship was the turning point in Irina and Aleksei's relationship; after that, they began to grow apart, even though they continued to skate together through 1972. "The hours of training became, more and more, a critical affair," Irina wrote in *Uneven Ice*. "In those days, I didn't feel free at all."

The time after her split with Aleksei was the worst in Irina's young life. But at her coach's urging, she pulled herself together and they started to search for a new partner. Finally, Alexandr Zaitsev, a skater from Leningrad, was chosen. At 5'10", he was almost a foot taller than Irina, and he turned out to be an even better skater and partner than Aleksei. When Irina and Sasha, as Alexandr was called, went to their summer training camp, they too fell in love. Irina and Sasha skated so

NEIL LEIFER/SPORTS ILLUSTRATED

well together that in their first season together they won the 1973 world championship, despite the fact that their music had accidentally stopped just after they had started their free skating program. They wanted to win the championship so badly that they continued their program without music, skating in unison. They shadowed one another's jumps, and Sasha lifted Irina in a perfect rhythm to music that only they could hear. They could have stopped and started over with their music, but Irina and Aleksei feared they would be marked down by the judges if they didn't keep going. The judges marked them as if the music had played, and Irina and Sasha won their first world championship together. They won the world championships again in 1974 and 1975. And in April of 1975, they were married.

In 1974, the couple had switched coaches. For several years, Irina had not liked working with Stanislav Zhuk, and when it became clear that Sasha and Mr. Zhuk did not get along, they began to work with Tatiana Tarasova. Ms. Tarasova was the daughter of the former Soviet hockey coach. She also knew the importance of drama and music in pairs skating. Most important, she was more easygoing than Zhuk had been. She encouraged Irina and Sasha to take their style in a new direction. She wanted to emphasize musicality in their artistic presentation, rather than the run-and-jump style of Zhuk.

That subtle change did not hurt Irina and Sasha's championship form. They won their first Olympic gold medal together at the 1976 Games in Innsbruck, Austria.

Irina and Sasha were so good and so thoroughly dominated pairs skating that in a way they almost ruined the sport. Competitions became predictable: Whenever Irina and Sasha skated, they won. And because there were no other couples who could beat them, many pairs skaters retired from amateur competition earlier than they might have. Irina and Sasha never made mistakes, and the difference in their heights enabled them to perform a variety of difficult lifts. They even took risks; Irina, for example, became the first woman to perform a double Axel jump in a pairs program. Irina and Sasha had a

feel for music and for one another, and these qualities came across in their skating.

In 1978, Irina won her 10th world championship. It was her sixth with Sasha, and it was her last. The following year, Irina and Sasha took a year off to have a baby. In the early part of 1979, Irina gave birth to a boy, also named Sasha.

Their year off was, in many ways, the best thing that could have happened to figure skating, because it allowed another couple to rise to prominence. That duo was Tai Babilonia and Randy Gardner, young pairs skaters from California. They had been third in the 1977 and 1978 world championships and had won the 1979 world championship. Tai and Randy were one of the first pairs to regularly perform dangerous throw moves, in which Randy would toss Tai across the ice to perform jumps. The throws could cause knee injuries if the woman skater didn't land correctly. For that reason, Irina and Sasha never included them in their programs.

Tai and Randy made pairs skating exciting to watch. Fans realized that Tai and Randy were a couple who could challenge Irina and Sasha. Many people looked forward to the 1980 Olympics, in Lake Placid, New York, hoping that Tai and Randy would score an upset.

Those people underestimated Irina and Sasha. They were stimulated by the competition from Tai and Randy and worked new moves into their traditional routines. In one of the new moves, Sasha lifted Irina above his head and moved her from a back press position to a tabletop position, as he skated quickly along the ice.

The showdown between the American and Russian team, however, never came off. A couple of weeks before the Olympics began, Randy pulled a muscle in his right thigh. He thought it had healed, but only a few days before the competition began, he pulled it again and injured another muscle as well. On the day of the short program competition, a doctor gave Randy a shot to numb the pain. But that last-minute effort couldn't save Randy from what was to come. When he and Tai went out to warm up for their short program, he fell

TONY TRIOLO/SPORTS ILLUSTRATED

good for the sport. The Americans' withdrawal virtually assured Irina and Sasha of their second gold medal together. The couple easily won the short program, earning scores of 5.8

Irina's 3 gold medals and 10 world titles, won with Aleksei and Sasha (shown), matched Sonja Henie's singles record.

or 5.9 from eight of the nine judges.

In the long program, which counted for 75 percent of the total score, Irina and Sasha skated to Russian folk music. Their program included exciting overhead lifts and side-by-side double flip jumps. What it did not include, however, was a death spiral. Irina and Sasha could perform stunning death spirals, and the judges were not pleased that they hadn't included one. Nonetheless, Irina and Sasha were so much better than their competition that they received the first place votes of all nine judges.

As the two received their gold medals in the awards ceremony, Irina could not hold back her tears. How different this ceremony was from the one in 1972 in Sapporo, Japan, where her heart had been broken. Here, in Lake Placid, Irina was overwhelmed by the joy she felt from her long and successful career, as well as from her happy marriage.

After this Olympics, she and Sasha would retire and become skating coaches in the Soviet Union. But as Irina savored this last victory, she thought about all that she had accomplished and how lucky she had been. Only the great Sonja Henie had accomplished as much: 10 world championships and three Olympic gold medals. Even with the broken heart she had suffered early in her career, it had all been worth it.

not once or twice, but *three* times on easy jumps. Randy had always been a superb jumper, and it was obvious that something was very wrong.

After watching Randy, the pair's coach, John Nicks, knew he had to withdraw the two from competition. He realized that if Randy's right leg collapsed while he was holding Tai above his head, Tai could be seriously injured. The coach could not take that chance.

When Tai and Randy learned that they would not be competing, Tai burst into tears. They had skated together for nine years and knew that this would be their last Olympics. It was a bitter way for their amateur careers to end.

Irina and Sasha were not happy that Tai and Randy had dropped out. The two couples were friendly, and both knew that their competition was

CHAPTER 17

Torvill and Dean

Stretching rules and imaginations made them ice dancing's greatest entertainers

When British ice dancers Jayne Torvill and Christopher Dean skated, they created their own form of magic. They experimented with music and moves, and performed with a passion and originality that the sport of ice dancing had never known. They often stretched the rules along the way, but no one seemed to care. That was because Torvill and Dean were more than good ice dancers. Sometimes, they were *perfect*.

Ice dancing is not quite art, and not quite sport. At its most basic level, it is the performance of ballroom dances—such as the waltz, tango, and polka—on ice. Just as in pairs skating, a man and a woman perform together, but they aren't allowed as much freedom. Ice dancers must stay within two arms' lengths of one another, and they are not allowed to be apart for more than five seconds at a time. They aren't permitted to do full-turn jumps and they may not perform lifts in which the man's arms are higher than his shoulders. They are also required to interpret their music, and it was here that

Torvill and Dean really stretched the rules.

When Jayne Torvill and Christopher Dean met, in 1974, neither seemed destined to take this then stodgy event to another level. They met at an ice rink in Nottingham, an English city about 110 miles north of London. Jayne was a clerk at an insurance company, and Christopher was a rookie policeman. They both came from working-class families; Christopher is the son of an electrician, and Jayne's parents owned a small newsstand and magazine shop, and lived in the apartment above it.

Torvill and Dean's original routines broke with ice dancing tradition, and earned them perfect scores.

Jayne, who was 17 at the time, and Christopher, who was 16, didn't hit it off immediately. On the ice, they thought they were physically mismatched. Jayne, at 5'½" tall, seemed too short for Christopher's 5'10", and Christopher, at 155 pounds, seemed too thin and weak to lift Jayne. Nonetheless, they decided to try skating as a team.

GRAHAM FINLAYSON/SPORTS ILLUSTRATED

Both had skated since they were 10, but with only moderate success. Jayne had won the junior British pairs championship in 1970 and the seniors in 1971 with partner Michael Hutchison. Christopher had won the British primary dance championship in 1972. But neither had won anything in international competition. By teaming up, they had nothing to lose.

Torvill and Dean began to practice together often. They had to train very early in the morning—from 4 a.m. to 6 a.m.—so that they could

GRAHAM FINLAYSON/SPORTS ILLUSTRATED

get to their jobs afterward.

Although they skated as if they were passionately in love, off the ice Jayne and Christopher were just friends.

The more they skated together, the more they realized that they were perfectly suited to one another. Other people began to think so, too; they had a rare chemistry that made them exciting to watch. In 1978, Torvill and Dean won the British ice dancing championship, the first of six British championships they would win.

In 1980, Torvill and Dean decided to quit their jobs and devote their lives to skating. They planned to live on as little money as possible, sacrificing a comfortable life for what they hoped would be future success. They didn't have to scrimp for long, though. That same year, the Nottingham city coun-

cil voted to give them a grant worth about $20,000 a year for training expenses.

They competed in the 1980 European and world championships, placing fourth in those events. They also skated at the 1980 Olympics in Lake Placid, New York, and finished fifth. The Soviet team of Natalia Linichuk and Gennady Karponosov won the gold medal. After the Olympics, the Soviet team, and the three teams who had finished right behind them, retired from the sport. And that's when Torvill and Dean's domination of ice dancing began.

In 1981, Torvill and Dean became the first non-Russian couple since 1969 to win an ice dancing world championship. They skated a conventional ice dancing routine—meaning that their music consisted of four songs, each with a different rhythm—to win the title. Ice dancers almost always use a combination of four songs, in order to show off the different tempos of skating that are required by the judges. But Torvill and Dean thought that the four-song tradition limited the artistic elements of ice dancing. The 1981 world championship was the last time they bothered to follow that tradition.

After the world championships, Christopher and Jayne began training with their coach, Betty Callaway, in Oberstdorf, West Germany, a small town on the border of the Austrian Alps. There, the three worked in almost complete secrecy, and began to experiment with music and new moves.

At the 1982 world championships, they unveiled their new program, in which they skated to only one piece of music, the overture from the Broadway play *Mack and Mabel*. The play was about a difficult love affair, and Torvill and Dean skated as though they were the couple in love. Despite the unconventional use of only one piece of music, the judges approved of their performance, and Torvill and Dean won their second world championship.

Their romantic style of skating made people wonder whether Torvill and Dean were in love in real life, as well. They weren't. "Love?" Christopher once said. "A romantic commitment would destroy everything we have worked for." Even so, the appearance on ice that they were deeply in love made their performances all the more dramatic and exciting.

Torvill and Dean's quest was for artistic and athletic perfection. Like all artists, Christopher wanted to push his art to its limits. Jayne shared his enthusiasm. Christopher choreographed almost all of their routines, although he always gave Jayne equal credit. "The idea," Jayne told *Sports Illustrated* in 1984, "is to take an ordinary sports event and bring to it a sense of *occasion*." Said Christopher, "We turn on the music and try to lead the audience into fantasy."

Before they met, Jayne and Christopher had had little success as skaters, but together they were golden.

TONY TOMSIC/SPORTS ILLUSTRATED

The free skating program that they introduced at the 1983 world championships in Helsinki, Finland, was a fantasy, indeed. Torvill and Dean called the program "Barnum on Ice," after P.T. Barnum, the founder of the Barnum & Bailey Circus. During their four-minute performance, they brought all the fun of a circus to the ice, pretending that they were tumblers, jugglers, tightrope walkers, and clowns.

Even though their routine included one lift in which Christopher's hand appeared to be over his shoulder (which is considered illegal), the judges saw nothing but perfection. All nine judges awarded the British team 5.9's for technical merit. Then, for the first time in skating history, every single judge awarded them a 6.0 for artistic impression. In their third world championship victory, Torvill and Dean were perfect!

Torvill and Dean collected perfect scores like some people collect baseball cards. No matter how many medals they won, though, they continued to push themselves. "Each year we try to be original and different," Christopher told the *Los Angeles Times* before the 1984 Olympics. "I think that's what people want to see, the anticipation of some-

thing new." The duo competed mostly against themselves; they never worried about their competition because they had none. At home in England, people called Torvill and Dean "Their Greatnesses."

They lived up to the title at the 1984 Olympics in Sarajevo, Yugoslavia. On the third day of Olympic competition, Torvill and Dean competed in the compulsories, in which skaters perform three required dances. The compulsories counted for 30 percent of the skaters' final score. The dances chosen for the Olympics were the rhumba, the Westminster waltz, and the *paso doble*. Torvill and Dean easily won the compulsories, receiving perfect scores of 6.0 from three of the nine judges for their interpretation of the Westminster waltz. They were the first couple in Olympic history to be awarded perfect scores for a compulsory dance.

The second event in ice dancing is the Original Set Pattern, which counted for 20 percent of the total score and is similar to singles skating's short program. Torvill and Dean won that event, too, receiving four 6.0's.

On the night of the free skating competition, which counted for 50 percent of the total score, all 8,500 seats of Sarajevo's Zetra ice arena were filled. In Great Britain, the British Broadcasting Company delayed its national news program to televise Torvill and Dean's performance.

For their long program, Torvill and Dean skated to the music of *Bolero,* by French composer Maurice Ravel. Their dance told the story of two doomed lovers who hurl themselves into a volcano so that they can be together in death. The music was very slow, very passionate, and it contained no dramatic change of tempo. Some people criticized Torvill and Dean for using single-tempo music; others thought that the program would be too bold and too different for the ice dancing judges. "Maybe it's something that hasn't been done before," Christopher had told *Time* magazine, "but that's what we're all about, trying to be inventive and to do different things. We didn't know how the music would be received, but we felt very strongly about it, and we stayed with that commitment."

When Torvill and Dean began, all criticism was silenced. Wearing purple outfits, the couple began their routine on their knees in an embrace. They stayed on their knees for a full 20 seconds. Then Christopher pulled Jayne over his shoulder and placed her gently on the ice. They performed a number of slow turns with their knees locked together, touching one another, and, once, kissing like the doomed lovers of their music.

Over the course of the program, Torvill and Dean performed difficult—but legal—lifts and arm twists. Near the end, Christopher swung Jayne around several times, as if he were throwing her into the fires of a volcano. Then they both threw themselves onto the ice as though making their suicide leaps. It was a dramatic ending for a program that had been pure passion. The judges awarded Torvill and Dean six 5.9's and three 6.0's for technical merit. For artistic impression, they received a row of solid 6.0's! They were the first skaters in any event to receive perfect scores from all judges in an Olympic event. Naturally, they won the gold medal as well.

Shortly after the Olympics, Torvill and Dean turned professional. They skated with their own ice show for several years, and later, as guests with the Ice Capades. They continued to take ice dancing in new directions, choreographing routines for themselves and for other ice dancers. In the 1990 NutraSweet Professional Championships, for example, they performed the required rhythm dance without music. Off the ice, Jayne married Phil Christensen, an American sound engineer she met when he worked on the 1989 Torvill and Dean U.S. tour. And Christopher married Isabelle Duchesnay, a Canadian ice dancer who, with her brother, Paul, won the 1991 world title. Christopher also works as the Duchesnays' choreographer.

After Torvill and Dean left amateur ice dancing, officials became stricter about enforcing the rules. As much as the judges had liked Torvill and Dean's *Bolero* program, they felt it was too modern. The judges wanted to discourage other ice dancers from trying experimental routines. This trend saddened Torvill and Dean, who had worked so hard to bring new life to their sport.

The judges can never, though, take away the joy that people felt when they watched Torvill and Dean skate. They will always be remembered for their creative and beautiful performances, and for their technical perfection. "Watching them skate, the way they caress the ice," said Bernard Ford, an earlier British ice dancing champion and four-time world champion, "it's like watching God skate."

About the Author

Laura Hilgers was part of the inaugural staff at SPORTS ILLUS-TRATED FOR KIDS Magazine. Her first SI FOR KIDS book was a biography of tennis star Steffi Graf. Writing *Great Skates* brought back memories of her childhood. When her family lived in Minnesota, Laura spent lots of time on the ice. She had a skating rink in her backyard and a public rink two blocks away. She still loves skating but, unlike the "great skates" in her book, she doesn't do any fancy moves when she's on the ice. Laura prefers to skate slowly and surely.

Blairsville High School Library